# history at source

# THE FRENCH REVOLUTION

## *1789-99*

### E G Rayner and R F Stapley

Hodder & Stoughton

A MEMBER OF THE HODDER HEADLINE GROUP

# ACKNOWLEDGEMENTS

The publishers wish to thank the following for permission to reproduce illustrations in this volume: Cover - Le Sueur Brothers, *Planting the Tree of Liberty*, The Bridgeman Art Library.
Hulton-Deutsch, p. 14; Musée Carnavalet, Paris / © SPADEM p. 20; The Syndics of Cambridge University Library / The Granger Collection, p. 40; Musée de la Ville de Paris / © SPADEM, p. 43; Bridgeman Art Library, p. 75 and p. 84; National Museums and Galleries on Merseyside / Walker Art Gallery, p. 85.

The publishers also wish to thank the following for their permission to reproduce material in this volume: Cambridge University Press for the extract from Martyn Lyons, *France Under The Directory* (1975); Routledge for the extracts from Gwynne Lewis, *The French Revolution: Rethinking the Debate* (1993).

Every effort has been made to trace and acknowledge ownership of copyright. The publishers will be glad to make suitable arrangements with any copyright holders whom it has not been possible to contact.

**British Library Cataloguing in Publication Data**
Rayner, E.G.
French Revolution, 1789-99. - (History
at Source Series)
I. Title II. Stapley, R.F. III Series
944.04

ISBN 0 340 62704 2


First published 1995
Impression number    10  9 8 7 6 5 4 3 2 1
Year                 1998  1997  1996  1995

Copyright © 1995 EG Rayner and RF Stapley

Typeset by Sempringham publishing services, Bedford
Printed in Great Britain for Hodder and Stoughton Educational, a division of Hodder Headline Plc, 338 Euston Road, London NW1 3BH by Page Bros (Norwich) Ltd

# CONTENTS

# PREFACE

The French Revolution still remains one of the most important topics in modern history, and as such has had little difficulty in maintaining its position at the heart of academic study and research. Many books have been written on the subject, and it has long remained a popular topic with students studying at A level, AS level, Higher Grade and beyond. At the same time, changes in the requirements of examination boards, particularly the introduction of source-based (*'common core'*) questions, coursework and personal assignments, have increased the demands on both students and teachers. The subject is too vast for this book to provide a continuous narrative of a very detailed and complex period. Hence it has a deliberately selective approach, taking a number of topics, and approaching them through selections of historical sources, concluding each selection with the type of questions likely to be encountered in examinations involving the use of sources. The selection of the documents does not pretend to be the final one. It is important for students who want to know the truth about what happened to read and consider carefully the views of historians as well as look at selections of documents. It is true that such views are secondary, but that fact by no means invalidates them.

Those students who feel the need for a firmer chronological framework, or whose factual knowledge of this difficult period is shaky, must also have alongside them in their work a historical text arranged along more conventional lines such as Duncan Townson's *France in Revolution,* in the *Access to History* series, also published by Hodder and Stoughton (1990). For the most part, this present book is topic and problem based, though there is a broad chronological sequence in its material. It offers practical advice on the way to tackle examination questions, and a specimen answer is provided. Guidance is also given on the writing of essay answers. Sample essay questions are given, together with suggestions for appropriate treatment; and again a specimen essay is included. Finally a bibliography is given in order to help students and teachers with available books.

It is hoped that this collection will prove useful for those working as part of an organised course or studying on their own without the help of a teacher.

# APPROACHING SOURCE-BASED

## QUESTIONS

Source-based questions have become an important part of History examinations at all levels in recent years. Students who have studied History at GCSE and Standard Grade will be used to handling various types of sources. The skills they have learned in dealing with evidence will continue to be applicable at a more advanced level, but there will also be more sophisticated skills to master, and the sources themselves will certainly be more demanding.

During your studies you will encounter both primary and secondary historical evidence. The difference between the two is sometimes artificially exaggerated: all sources have their value and limitations, and it is possible to worry unnecessarily about a 'hierarchy of sources'. The important thing is for the student to feel confident in handling all sources. The majority of sources in this book are primary sources, since they are the raw material from which historians work; and they are mostly of a documentary nature, because that is the type most commonly found in examinations. However there are also examples of visual evidence. The comments below apply to all types of evidence.

When students are faced with a piece of historical evidence, there are certain questions that they should always ask of that source; but in an examination the student will be asked specific questions set by an examiner, and, in the light of pressures - not least of which is time - it is important to approach these questions in an organised and coherent fashion.

The following advice should be borne in mind when answering source-based questions. Some of the advice may seem obvious in the cold light of day, but, as examiners will testify, the obvious is often forgotten in the heat of the examination room!

## *Answering documentary questions*

1 Skim through all the documents quickly, making sure you have read all of them and that there are no others over the page. When you have done this, and decided that this is a question which you may attempt, read them through again, more carefully and slowly, taking in their overall meaning.

2 Pay particular attention to the *attribution* of each source, noting its author, date and place of origin. Note whether it is a document contemporary with the subject it deals with, or whether it is written later and with the benefit of hindsight. Note also why it was written; the context in which it is written, i.e. whether it is confidential or in the public domain; whether the author is an expert in the matter or merely an observer, and whether the recipient (if any)

stands in any special relationship with the author or is in any other way privileged. Note, too, whether the document is in the original language or is translated.

3 Read through all the sub-questions (or *items*) attached to the documents. Before you start a question, remember that the opening items may be deceptively simple, but that they may get harder in the later stages.

4 Study the tariff of marks on offer, and tailor the length of your answers accordingly. There is no point in writing a lengthy paragraph to score 1 mark; a short sentence, a phrase or even a single word may be enough. Nor can you be expected to score 4 or 5 marks if you write no more than a few words on a more heavily weighted item. Unnecessarily long answers should be avoided, but at the same time you should take care to provide enough 'meat' in your answer to warrant full marks.

5 Study the wording of the items closely. Some will ask you to use only your own knowledge in the answer; some will ask you to use both your knowledge and the sources; others will insist that you confine your answer to the knowledge gleaned from the sources alone. You will lose marks if you ignore these instructions.

6 In writing your answers, avoid irrelevant narrative. Use the document appropriately, and use brief quotations from it if this serves to reinforce your answer. If you are asked for a specific feature of the document, use the document for the answer. Do not rely on what you imagine the document ought to say, but what it actually does.

7 If there are several sources to be consulted, be sure you make use of the ones to which you are directed. Candidates have been known to omit some, or even to chose the wrong ones.

8 Certain types of question require a particular type of response:
   (a) comparison of sources: be sure that you compare all the sources asked for.
   (b) commenting on the usefulness and limitations of sources: if asked to do both, be sure that you consider both aspects.
   (c) commenting on reliability: this is not the same as commenting on the usefulness of a source, although the two are sometimes confused.
   (d) responding to requests to 'analyse' or 'assess' the content of the sources. Always use the sources and do not just copy what is in front of you. What is wanted is a considered judgment.
   (e) synthesis: a high-level skill which requires you to bring together several pieces of evidence and draw an overall conclusion.

9 Avoid spending too much of your time on the sources questions in examinations. The amount of time you should spend should depend on the proportion of marks allocated to them in the paper.

10 If possible, read the published examiners' reports which give you further
information on the most useful approaches to adopt, and pitfalls to avoid.

## Some useful vocabulary

Authenticity: Is the document genuine, or is it a fraud?
Reliability:  Is the document truthful, or is it misleading?
Validity:     Is the document logically sound, or are the conclusions being
              drawn from it not supported by the evidence it provides?
Usefulness:   Does the document cast important light on its subject, or is it
              only of marginal importance?

Examples:

1 A letter supposedly written by Louis XVI inviting foreign princes to invade
France, but actually forged by one of his accusers at the time of his trial, is
not *authentic*, but *is false*.

2 The story that Marie Antoinette had hundreds of pairs of shoes is *not reliable
evidence* of her extravagance; for a queen, this would not have been unusual.

3 The suggestion that since Danton was very popular in Paris in 1794 he was
innocent of all the charges Robespierre brought against him is not *valid;* if
his guilt was secret his popularity would not suffer.

4 The fact that Robespierre did not have time to powder his wig on the day of
his execution is not *important;* personal tidiness was the least of his concerns
at that time.

## A Note on this Collection of Sources

This collection aims to give ideas to teachers and realistic examples of sources
and questions to students, either for use in schools and colleges, or for
self-study. They are intended to be flexible. If it is helpful, adapt the questions
and mark allocations, or devise new questions; or use the sources as part of
coursework or personal studies. You might even find it useful to put together
your own sources, and to write the appropriate questions for them.

## Timeline

### Pre-1789

| | | |
|---|---|---|
| 1774 | Accession of Louis XVI | |
| 1774-6 | Ministry of Turgot | |
| 1781 | Compte Rendu. Dismissal of Necker | |
| 1783 | Calonne Controller General | End of American War of Independence |

1787    Assembly of Notables
1788    Calonne replaced by de Brienne
        Recall of Necker
        Second Assembly of Notables
        The 'Result of the Council'

---

### 1789

| | |
|---|---|
| 5 May | Estates General opened at Versailles |
| 17 June | National Assembly proclaimed |
| 20 June | Tennis Court Oath |
| 23 June | Three Estates ordered to separate |
| 27 June | Union of the Three Estates |
| 11 July | Necker again dismissed |
| 12-14 July | Formation of National Guard |
| | Storming of the Bastille |
| July/August | Great Fear |
| 4 August | 'Abolition' of feudalism in France |
| 26 August | Declaration of Rights of Man |
| 5 October | March of the Women to Versailles |
| 2 November | Confiscation of Church Estates |

---

### 1790

| | | |
|---|---|---|
| April | First issue of assignats | |
| July | Civil Constitution of the Clergy | |
| Nov | Assembly imposes clerical oath | |
| Dec | King accepts clerical oath | Louis XVI in correspondence with foreign sovereigns |

### 1791

| | | |
|---|---|---|
| March | Pope condemns Civil Constitution | |
| April | Death of Mirabeau | |
| June | Flight to Varennes | |
| July | Massacre of the Champ de Mars | Padua Circular |
| | Aug | Declaration of Pillnitz |
| Sept | King accepts 1791 Constitution | |
| Oct | Legislative Assembly meets | |
| Nov | King vetoes decrees against émigrés | |
| Dec | King vetoes decrees against clergy | |

### 1792

| | | |
|---|---|---|
| March | Brissotin Ministry | |
| April | France declares war on Austria | |
| June | Tuileries invaded by Parisians | |
| July | First Feast of the Federation | Brunswick Manifesto |
| Aug | Insurrectionary Commune set up | |

Paris Insurrection and attack on the Tuileries
Fall of Monarchy
King a prisoner in the Temple
Sept    Prison massacres in Paris            Capture of Verdun by Prussians
National Convention meets              Battle of Valmy. Prussians retreat
Battle of Jemappes
Austrian defeat

Republic proclaimed
Oct     Committee of General Security
Nov/Dec Edicts of Fraternity

## 1793

Jan     Trial and Execution of King
Feb     France declares war on Britain
March   Outbreak of Vendéan revolt          France declares war on Spain
Revolutionary Tribunal set up          France defeated at Neerwinden
April   Committee of Public Safety set up   Desertion of Dumouriez
May     First Law of the Maximum
June    Fall of the Girondins
July    Revolutionary Tribunal reorganised
Assassination of Marat                 Fall of Mainz to Prussians
Aug     Levée en Masse                      Toulon surrendered to English
Sept    Law of General Maximum
Oct     Execution of Queen
Execution of Girondins
'Government is revolutionary until the peace'
Nov     Revolutionary Calendar adopted
'Feast of Reason' in Notre Dame
Dec     Collapse of Vendéan rising          Toulon recaptured from English

## 1794

March   Execution of Hébert and supporters
Laws of Ventôse
April   Execution of Danton and supporters
May     Festival of the Supreme Being
June    Law of Prairial                     Battle of Fleurus. French occupy
Belgium
July                                        End of foreign threat
Fall and execution of Robespierre
Oct     Collapse of First Coalition
Nov     Jacobin Club closed
Dec     Law of Maximum repealed

## 1795

April   *Journée* of Germinal               Prussia makes peace at Basel
May     *Journée* of Prairial               Holland makes peace at The
Hague
June    Louis XVII dies in prison           Royalist invasion, Quiberon Bay
July                                        Invasion defeated
Spain makes peace with France

| | | | |
|---|---|---|---|
| Aug | Law of the Two-Thirds | | |
| | Constitution of 1795 (Year III) | | |
| Oct | Rising of Vendémiaire crushed | | |
| | Directory takes over power | | |
| | | Nov | Belgium annexed by France |

**1796**

| | | | |
|---|---|---|---|
| March | *Mandats territoriaux* issued | | Start of Bonaparte's Italian campaign |
| | | April | Piedmont makes Truce of Cherasco |
| May | Conspiracy of Equals | | Bonaparte defeats Austrians at Lodi |
| | | Nov | Victory of Arcola |
| | | Dec | French invasion of Ireland foiled |

**1797**

| | | | |
|---|---|---|---|
| | | Jan | Victory of Rivoli |
| | | April | French occupation of Venice |
| | | | Preliminaries of Léoben |
| May | Execution of Babeuf | | Treaty of Milan with Venice |
| | | June | Ligurian Republic set up |
| | | | Cisalpine Republic set up |
| Sept | Coup of Fructidor | | |
| | Law of the Consolidated Third | | |
| | | Oct | Treaty of Campo Formio with Austria |
| | | | End of Italian Campaign |

**1798**

| | | | |
|---|---|---|---|
| | | April | Helvetic Republic set up |
| May | Coup of Floréal | | Bonaparte captures Malta |
| | | June | Start of Egyptian Campaign |
| | | July | Battle of the Pyramids |
| | | | French occupy Cairo |
| | | Aug | Battle of Aboukir Bay |
| Sept | France adopts general conscription | | |
| | | Nov | Naples attacks Roman Republic |
| | | | Second Coalition formed |

**1799**

| | | | |
|---|---|---|---|
| | | March | France declares war on Austria |
| May | Sieyès joins the Directory | | |
| June | Coup of Prairial | | |
| July | Law of Hostages | | |
| | | Aug-Sept | France defeated in Netherlands and Italy |
| Oct | Bonaparte returns from Egypt | | |
| Nov | Coup of 18 Brumaire | | |
| | Consulate established | | |

# 1 THE INTELLECTUAL BACKGROUND
## TO THE FRENCH REVOLUTION

The French Revolution is usually said to have owed something to the ideas of the eighteenth-century Enlightenment as they were expressed by the philosophic movement operating in France in that century.

Most of the philosophers of the Enlightenment lived in the earlier part of the eighteenth century, and did not survive to see the coming of the Revolution. If they had, they would have probably been aghast at the interpretations that were put on their words, and the lengths to which their ideological principles were stretched. One survivor was Condorcet, who served for a time in the Revolutionary government under the Girondins, and was responsible for recommending a major reorganisation of the French educational system; he found himself increasingly out of sympathy with the Paris radicals, fled in order to escape the guillotine, but died in prison in 1794.

Some later interpretations of the philosophic movement have laid great stress on the impact of intellectual theories on the Revolution, suggesting that it was the ferment of ideas during the Enlightenment which provided the engine for much of its revolutionary momentum. Others have dismissed the movement altogether in a few contemptuous phrases, or have relegated its importance to a subsidiary level. These take the view that the Revolution was mainly brought about by the institutional weakness of the government of the ancien régime, or by impending financial bankruptcy; ideas played only a secondary role. Marxist historians contend that the bourgeoisie seized on the ideas of the enlightenment as ammunition with which to bombard the entrenched positions of the French ruling class, so enforcing the claims to political dominance to which, in a capitalist society, they believed their wealth and their influence entitled them.

## A Contemporary Reactions to the Philosophic Writings of the Eighteenth Century

(i) The books containing these pernicious ideas are endlessly produced before our eyes. We have even had the misfortune to see some of them in books produced under the seal of official authority. Other works, though more furtively produced, are snapped up with no less enthusiasm. Mercenary writers, dispensing with the morality both of Church and State, shamefully traffic in the highest and most noble of ideals. Printers, equally criminal and greedy, lend all the supports of their arts to these writers: poisons, concocted by some and spread by

8

others, together with the venality of the hands distributing them, ensure the prevalence of the infection.

from a speech by the Bishop of Puy, in the Assembly of the Clergy, protesting against the failure of the Royal Government to enforce censorship laws (1752)

(ii) There is a great outcry against the *Encyclopedia,* and this outcry comes from the Jesuits, staging a great quarrel with the authors of that work... And what are they saying against the authors of this great and useful work? They are accusing them of impiety. The *Encyclopedia* is threatened with being attacked and banned. They say the book is the haunt of the members of this impious cult. This is a frightful onslaught against the century's most talented writers, threatening them once again with the repression of Jesuitry... What will follow will be the loss of many excellent men of letters from France, an event which will enrich envious neighbours. Worse still, the end result in France will be the establishment of a veritable Inquisition, one which the Jesuits will happily take charge of, one which they have long worked for and which they will rigorously carry out... Secular tyranny is in an unholy alliance with ecclesiastical tyranny.

from the Count d'Argenson, defending the *Encyclopedia* and the other work of the philosophes (1752)

(iii) When once a nation begins to think it is impossible to prevent it. This century has seen the beginnings of the triumph of reason; the Jesuits, the Jansenists, the hypocrites of the legal profession and of the Court have protested against it in vain, and have excited in honest folk no more than horror and scorn. It is in the King's own interest that the number of the philosophers increase and that of fanatics diminish. We are the peaceful ones, and it is people like them who are the stirrers; we are the solid citizens, they the treasonable ones; we nurture reason in peace and they persecute it; they seek to have a number of good books burned, whilst we will obliterate them from society, destroying their credit in decent society; for it is only decent society which shapes the opinions of men.

from Letter to *Helvétius* by Voltaire (1760)

**B The Ideas of the Philosophers during the French Revolution**
We shall show how nature has joined together indissolubly the advance of knowledge and that of liberty, virtue and respect for the natural rights of man; and how these, though so often separated that they have even been held to be incompatible, must on the contrary become inseparable from the moment that enlightenment has attained a certain level... Once such a close accord has been established between all enlightened men, from then onwards all will be the

friends of humanity, and all will work together for its perfection and its happiness...

How consoling for the philosopher who laments the errors, the crimes and the injustices which still pollute the earth, is this view of the human race emancipated from its shackles, advancing with a firm and sure step along the path of truth. It is the contemplation of this prospect that rewards him for all his efforts to assist the progress of reason and the defence of liberty. Such contemplation is for him an asylum, in which the memories of his persecutors cannot pursue him; there he lives in thought with man restored to his natural rights and dignity, forgets man tormented and corrupted by greed, fear or envy; there he lives with his peers in an Elysium created by reason and graced by the purest pleasures known to the love of mankind.

from the Marquis de Condorcet, *Draft for a Historical Portrait of the Progress of the Human Spirit,* written before his death in prison in 1794

## C  A Modern View of the Eighteenth-century Philosophers

*Reason* was the word which tripped lightly off the tongue of most reformers: it was the word we most often associate with the Enlightenment. This is not to argue that the ideas of the Enlightenment 'caused' the French Revolution. The study of history should not be concerned with laying down single-track lines from one set of points to another, passing chronological stations *en route.* In the first place, most of the standard texts we associate with the Enlightenment had been published before Robespierre was born; in the second, the movement was extremely disparate and multi-faceted, with atheists, freemasons and Catholics all claiming to be 'enlightened.' The argument in Montesquieu's *Esprit des Lois* (1748) was relativist and élitist: different forms of government suited different countries; nobles, as represented in the *parlements,* provided a salutary check on royal despotism. Like Montesquieu, Voltaire had drunk deeply at the well of the English Enlightenment, associated in the main with the ideas of Locke and Newton. Living the life of a seigneur at Ferny near the Swiss border in the 1760s, this mocking sage had absolutely no love for the masses...

Far more radical then Montesquieu and Voltaire in their approach were the authors of the *Encyclopedia,* Denis Diderot and Jean d'Alembert: the former's brilliant analyses of French culture and society contained more than one whiff of modernity. If the classic works of Montesquieu and Voltaire had drawn their inspiration from the past, the articles published in the *Encyclopedia,* accompanied by state-of-the-art engravings and illustrations, pointed the way forward to a more rational, scientific and humane period in European history, one which our century has done little to advance...

Is it a coincidence that the high peak of the Enlightenment in the

1750s and 1760s coincided with a period of very considerable economic growth in France? Marxist historians such as Albert Soboul certainly posited an *indirect* relationship between the widely perceived growth of capitalism and the intellectual 'take-off' of the Enlightenment: 'the philosophers explained that man must try to understand nature so that he could more effectively control it and so increase the general wealth of the community'.[1] For Marxist scholars, socio-economic change provides the soil in which the seeds of the Enlightenment could germinate.

Note 1. Albert Soboul, *The French Revolution, 1787-99: From the Storming of the Bastille to Napoleon*, 1989. p. 28.

from Gwynne Lewis, *The French Revolution: Rethinking the Debate* (1993)

## Questions

1 'For an autocratic régime, pre-revolutionary France was remarkably tolerant of subversive literature.' How far do Sources A and C support this view? **(5 marks)**

2 In what ways do the Bishop of Puy's arguments in A(i) differ from those of Voltaire in A(iii)? How do you explain these differences? **(8 marks)**

3 'Source B could well have been from a contemporary speech by Robespierre.' How far do you agree? Use the source and your own knowledge to develop your answer. **(8 marks)**

4 'The Enlightenment in France was generally in sympathy with, rather than hostile to, the growth of capitalism.' Do you agree? Use the sources and your own knowledge to develop your answer. **(9 marks)**

# 2 THE PEASANT ORIGINS
## OF THE FRENCH REVOLUTION

There is general agreement that the French peasant played a very important part in bringing about and sharing in the action of the French Revolution. At the time when the National Assembly was being created in Paris in the summer of 1789 the peasants were staging a rebellion of their own directed against their seigneurs and what remained of the feudal regime.

To explain these actions, two contrasting scenarios have been put forward. One explanation is that the Revolution sprang from the poverty, misery and suffering of the French nation, ground down by the hopelessness and exploitation that the people were compelled to suffer. This was the view put forward at the time and immediately afterwards, and is a view for which there is much evidence. At the same time, it should be remembered that few peasants, then or now, make a great display of their wealth; furthermore, their desire for owning land was little short of an obsession and most were happy to impoverish themselves in order to get more of it. The opposing view is that for much of the eighteenth century, output was increasing, wealth was accumulating, trade and industry were progressing and standards of living were rising - but unevenly, and not fast enough to satisfy popular aspirations. Many people noted the improvements but grew impatient that they were coming too slowly, with the result that expectations exceeded achievements, and the lower classes became more discontented with their lot.

Some historians took one side of the argument, some the other; but both groups were generalising from particular sets of facts. The great change came with two groups of writers in the twentieth century, both of which placed their emphasis on the need for detailed research on social and economic aspects of the Revolution at the most basic level. The first group included C.A. Labrousse, who believed that economic changes were not determined by a few simple factors, but by a vast complex of matters such as prices, real and nominal wages, rents, modes of production, degree of industrialisation, and so on, and who therefore brought into play an impressive range of statistical techniques to arrive at a genuinely scientific and objective treatment of the problem. The other group was the Marxist school, some of whom, like Georges Lefebvre, avoided generalisations and concentrated on detailed regional studies in order to get closer to the truth. Whereas one approached the problem by abstracting a limited number of crucial features of the problem and by attempting to study them on a nationwide scale, the other was limited to

12

a small geographical area and studied its society and economy in its totality and in all its variegated detail. Both ways were selective and avoided superficial generalisations; at the same time, both methods made final conclusions all the more difficult to reach.

## A  Contemporary Views on the Lot of the French Peasant

(i) To take the time of the labourer, even for pay, is the equivalent of a tax. To take this time without paying for it is a double tax, and one out of all proportion when it falls on the simple day-labourer who has nothing for his livelihood but the work of his hands.

The man who works under compulsion and without payment works idly and without interest; he does less work, and his work is badly done. Those who perform the corvée are forced to travel often ten miles or more to report to the foreman, and as much again to return to their homes, and so waste a good part of the time demanded from them without any return for it. The complaints, the embarrassment of tracing out the work, of distributing it, of executing it with a gang of men gathered together haphazard, most of them as devoid of intelligence as they are of initiative, consume a further part of the remaining time. In this way the work done costs the people and the state, in labour and vehicles, twice and often three times as much as what it would cost if it were done for a money consideration.

from A.R.J. Turgot, in the preamble to his *Edict on the Corvée* (1776)

(ii) Afflicted by so many misfortunes and suffering from poverty, the people of the countryside have become listless; they have fallen into a state of numbness, a kind of apathy, which is disastrous for the prosperity of the country. The population is suffering. They are afraid to get married, for marriage only holds the prospect of further hardships; they would immediately be taxed, asked for road services, for labour services and contributions of all kinds. They fear a situation where their family would be a burden on them, since they can only expect their children to be poor and wretched.

from the Cahier of Pleurs in the Bailliwick of Sézanne, 1789)

(iii) Good Heavens! Do all the wastes, the deserts, the heath, ling, furze, broom and bog that I have passed for three hundred miles lead to this spectacle? What a miracle, that all this splendour and wealth of the cities of France should be so unconnected with the country! There are no gentle transitions from ease to comfort, from comfort to wealth; you pass at once from beggary to profusion, from misery in mud cabins to Mlle. Saint-Huberty, in splendid displays at 500 livres a night.

from *Travels in France* by Arthur Young (1788-9)

(iv) **The Peasant Crushed by the Taille and the Corvée**

## B   Later Views on the Economic Background to the Revolution
(i) The evil consists in this, that the nation, from the highest to the lowest, is organised so as to go on producing less and less, and paying more and more. She will go on declining, wasting away, giving, after her blood, her marrow; and there will be no end to it...

The peasant having no goods to seize, the Exchequer can lay hold of nothing but the cattle; it is gradually exterminated. No more manure. The cultivation of corn, though extended in the seventeenth century by immense clearings of waste land, decreases in the eighteenth. The earth can no longer repair her generative strength; she fasts, and becomes exhausted.

from *History of the French Revolution* by Jules Michelet (1847)

(ii) A study of comparative statistics makes it clear that in none of the decades immediately following the Revolution did our national prosperity make such rapid forward strides as in the two preceding it...

At first sight it seems hard to account for this steady increase in the wealth of the country despite the as yet unremedied shortcomings

THE LIBRARY
GUILDFORD COLLEGE The Peasant Origins of the French Revolution
of Further and Higher Education

of the administration and the obstacles with which industry still had to contend... That France could prosper and grow rich, given the inequality of taxation, the vagaries of local laws, internal customs barriers, feudal rights, the trade corporations, the sales of offices, and all the rest, may well seem hardly credible. Yet the fact remains that the country did grow richer and living conditions improved throughout the land, and the reason was that though the machinery of government was ramshackle, ill regulated, inefficient, and though it tended to hinder rather than to further social progress, it had two redeeming features which sufficed to make it function and made for national prosperity. First, though the government was no longer despotic, it was still powerful and capable of maintaining order everywhere; and secondly, the nation possessed an upper class that was the freest, most enlightened of the day, and a social system under which every man could get rich if he set his mind to it, and keep intact the wealth he had acquired...

In 1780 there could no longer be any talk of France's being on the downgrade; on the contrary, it seemed that no limit could be set to her advance. And it was now that theories of the perfectibility of man and continuous progress came into fashion. Dazzled by the prospect of a felicity undreamed of hitherto and now within their grasp, people were blind to the very real improvement that had taken place and were eager to precipitate events.

from *The Old Régime and the French Revolution* by Alexis de Tocqueville (1856)

(iii) Tocqueville failed to notice what only recent research has brought to light: that in the closing years of the ancien régime that the general prosperity of agriculture was grinding to a halt. This developed in two stages. After 1778, the year France entered the American War, there was a recession as a result of which prices fell - gradually in most industrial and farm products, but reaching crisis proportions in wines and textiles. During these years, the profits of small tenant farmers, peasant proprietors, wine growers and other share-croppers tended, because of the heavy and sustained toll of tax, tithe and seigneurial exaction, to fall out of all proportion to the fall in prices, while large landed proprietors were cushioned against loss by means of their feudal revenues. Then, on top of this cyclical depression, came the sudden catastrophe of 1787-89, which took the form of bad harvests and shortage, with the price of wheat doubling within two years in the main productive regions of the north and reaching record levels in twenty-seven out of the thirty-two *généralités* in mid-summer 1789.

from *Europe in the Eighteenth Century: Aristocracy and the Bourgeois Challenge* by George Rudé (1972)

15

(iv) An infallible sign that the wealth of the country was increasing was that the population was growing rapidly and the prices of commodities, land and houses were steadily rising. Comfort was steadily spreading downwards, from the upper to the lower middle classes and that of artisans and small shopkeepers. People dressed better and had better food than in former days. Above all, education was spreading...

And so the Revolution was not to break out in an exhausted country but, on the contrary, in a flourishing land on a rising tide of progress. Poverty may sometimes lead to riots, but it cannot bring about great social upheavals. These always arise from a disturbance of the balance between the classes.

The middle classes certainly possessed the greater part of the fortune of France. They were advancing steadily, whereas the privileged orders were ruining themselves. Their very rise made them more acutely sensitive to the inferior legal status to which they were condemned. Barnave became a revolutionary the day that his mother was turned out of the box which she was occupying in the theatre at Grenoble by a nobleman. Mme. Roland complains that when she was asked to stay to dinner at the Château of Fontenoy with her mother, it was served to them in the servants' quarters. How many enemies of the old régime were made by wounded self-esteem!

from *The French Revolution* by Albert Mathiez (1928)

(v) In 1789 the French peasants already held a significant proportion of the soil of France; perhaps 30 to 40 per cent on the average, sometimes very much less, sometimes very much more... At the end of the Old Régime, furthermore, the population was increasing very fast and accordingly the agrarian crisis was growing more acute.

This is manifest by the ardour with which the peasants encroached on the common land or forests in order to build themselves a cottage or to clear small areas so as to add to their tillable land. The Cahiers very often demanded the sale or lease of portions of the royal domain or of the church lands... They called for the dividing up of the great leaseholds and large blocks of land rented to agricultural entre-preneurs for profit, or at least demanded that the number of small plots available be not decreased...

The consolidating of leasehold lands and the increase in the number of agricultural entrepreneurs who rented large tracts of land where share-cropping had previously prevailed was principally the work of the great proprietors... but perhaps the most curious and least noted feature of this situation was that the tightening up of the feudal régime which was an indisputable characteristic of the eighteenth century, and especially the second half, stemmed from the same source. To free himself from the bother of managing his own estates and to assure himself of an increasing or at least a constant income, the seigneur leased out the right to collect the income from his feudal rights just as he farmed out in a block the right to his half of the crop of his share-croppers, or consolidated his leases in the hands of a large-scale leaseholder...

With these facts in mind a few reflections of the greatest importance cannot fail to occupy our minds. The economic interpretation of history is given too narrow an interpretation when the French Revolution is made to evolve solely from the rise of the bourgeoisie. It arose also out of the resistance which the privileged classes opposed to the rise of the new economic order... But it had its origin equally in the opposition of the least favoured classes to the capitalistic order which had begun to be established.

from Georges Lefebvre, taken from two lectures at the Sorbonne and later printed in *Studies on the French Revolution*, 1932

# Questions

**1** (a) What do you understand by the taille and the corvée? **(6 marks)**
  (b) Explain the meaning of the engraving (Source A (iv)). **(4 marks)**

**2** 'As Arthur Young was English, his evidence is only of limited value.' Do you agree? **(4 marks)**

**3** Was de Tocqueville correct in saying that the government was 'no longer despotic' (Source B(ii))? Use your own knowledge of the ancien régime to develop your answer. **(8 marks)**

**4** To what extent do the other sources support or refute Lefebvre's view that capitalism, not feudalism, provoked the Revolution (Source B (v))? **(8 marks)**

# 3 ARISTOCRACY AND BOURGEOISIE IN THE FRENCH REVOLUTION

Two classes in pre-revolutionary France were broadly identifiable in their composition and outlook, and are reckoned to have had considerable influence on the course of events to 1789. These were the aristocracy and the bourgeoisie. Their interests are often said to have been opposed to each other, and there is clear contemporary evidence of mutual friction and hostility, as well as clear evidence of hostility to both of them on the part of the lower classes. The ambitions of these two classes helped in their different ways to bring about the start of the revolution. The role played by them – particularly by the bourgeoisie – in the Revolutionary and Napoleonic periods is also a vastly important one, providing ample opportunity for Marxist historians to see the period as one in which the capitalist bourgeoisie seized control of the political machine, thus providing another illustration of the Marxist interpretation of history.

Some historians, of course, laid the blame for the Revolution not on any cross-section or class of people in eighteenth-century France, but on groups of disaffected or malevolent individuals operating their own dark designs, perhaps not with a view to bringing down the whole system, but for more limited objectives. These groups were taken aback when events got out of hand, and some of them finished by regretting their original intentions. This was a 'theory of conspiracy' and was favoured by a number of early writers on the Revolution.

Most historians have concentrated their attention on the parts played by either the aristocracy or the bourgeoisie, and have attempted to show how different these two roles were. More recent analyses, however, have gone some way towards blurring the distinctions between them, showing how far they overlapped and intermingled, even perhaps suggesting that the supposed differences between them were more apparent than real. This has not negated Marxist theories, but has shown up the very theoretical terms in which the Marxist argument tends at present to be conducted.

## A Views on the French Aristocracy
(i) What spectacle more disturbing to behold for gentlemen of old extraction, often returned to their lands with honourable marks of their service and their courage, than to see at every turn their escutcheons mixing with those of persons who have barely had time to buy the right to possess them, and to find themselves compelled at church to share with those newcomers the honours which for several centuries have been rendered only to them [the real

gentlemen] and their ancestors.

from *The Remonstrance of the Paris Parlement* (1748)

(ii) The pride of wealth is different from the pride of birth. The one has something unconstrained about it which seems to elicit a legitimate admiration. The other has a revolting vulgarity which savours of usurpation.

from *Considerations on French Manners* by Charles Pinot Duclos (1787)

(iii) A sovereign can create princes; education, circumstances, genius can create heroes; none of these can produce a gentleman. Nobility remains a matter of blood.

from the Marquis de Custine, 1839

## B  Views on the French Bourgeoisie
(i) Finance today is allied with nobility, and that is the basis of its real power. The dowries of nearly all the lords' brides come from the fortunes of merchant houses. It is pleasant enough to see a count or a viscount, with nothing to him but a fine name, seeking out the rich daughter of a financier; and the financier, rolling in money, going to ask for a young lady of quality, bringing him nothing except her connection with an illustrious family.

   The difference is that the lady of rank (threatened with spending the rest of her life in a convent) regrets marrying a man with an investment income of five hundred thousand livres, reckons that she has done him a great favour by giving him her hand, and appeals to her ancestors' portraits to close their eyes to this misalliance. The foolish husband, quite puffed up with the privilege of dispensing his money amongst her parents and other hangers-on, thinks himself signally honoured to have lined the pockets of his haughty bride, pushing his acquiescence to the point of considering himself much beneath her. How despicable and foolish is the logic of vanity!

from *Portrait of Paris* by L.S. Mercier (1789)

(ii) On the sixteenth of this month there took place here the great marriage of the daughter of Presiding-judge Bernard de Rieux, grand-daughter of Samuel Bernard, to the Marquis of Mirepoix, of the house of Lévis de Ventadour. She was only twelve-and-a-half. Samuel Bernard gave her eight hundred thousand livres on her marriage. There was a splendid celebration. Plenty of people blamed the Marquis, who has getting on for thirty thousand livres of private income, for linking himself with a name so lowly and so disparaged as hers. But these days only money matters.

from Barbier's Journal, *Chronicle of the Regency and of the Reign of Louis XV* (1733)

**(iii) The bourgeoise mimicking the society lady**

## C   The Conspiracy Theory of the Revolution

Edmund Burke, though neither a Frenchman nor a historian, left in his *Reflections on the French Revolution* [1790ff] a record that has influenced the views of many people since. To Burke, French society was by no means antipathetic; in fact, it needed only a few adjustments to put it right. The Revolution could not therefore, in his opinion, be the outcome of a genuine and widespread feeling for reform, but rather of the machinations of the few: he instances, in particular, the clique of literary men and *philosophes* who had long been sniping at the established church, and the jumped-up moneyed interest, eager to settle accounts with the older aristocracy. And in the wake of these, he argued, followed the 'mob' or 'swinish multitude', eager for loot and incapable of holding any views of their own. Thus the Revolution, having no roots in legitimate dissatisfaction, was the child of the conspiracy of a few. This 'conspiracy' explanation... has found favour with many to whom the Revolution has appeared as an evil from start to finish and who have consequently, in order to explain its origins, fastened on a variety of scapegoats, including Freemasons, Jews, *illuminati,* Committees of Thirty, 'literary cabals' and disgruntled lawyers.

from *Europe in the Eighteenth Century: Aristocracy and the Bourgeois Challenge* by George Rudé (1972)

## D Some More Recent Views of the Struggle of Aristocracy v. Bourgeoisie

(i) Faced with the decline of French military power, many aristocrats looked for a remedy not to social change, but to a return to the old values which, they supposed, money had corrupted. They were prepared to make more concessions to the new values than is sometimes admitted. By 1789, they were prepared to give up their privileges in matters of taxation. But they were not prepared to give up their honorific privileges, including their right to sit separately from the Third Estate in the Estates General - for these were the badges of their order guaranteed them by law. They clung to the myths of blood and of the nobility as an estate; and they did so because they believed... that it was to these that France had owed her greatness.

from *The Ancien Régime* by C.B.A. Behrens (1967)

(ii) From 1760 onwards, the notions of worthiness and honour, which until then had defined what was special about nobles, were overtaken by a new notion: merit, a middle-class value, typical of the third order, which nobility took over, accepted and officially recognized as a criterion of nobility. From that moment on there was no longer any siginificant difference between nobility and middle class. A noble was now nothing but a commoner who had made it ...

To have access to education was not strictly a privilege of birth, but rather one of wealth. The rich middle classes also took advantage of it, and in the best schools the sons of tax-farmers rubbed shoulders with the sons of dukes and princes of the blood. In this way a cultural élite emerged in which old stock mingled with new blood, and magistrates-to-be with officers-to-be.

from *The French Nobility in the Eighteenth Century from Feudalism to Enlightenment* by G. Chaussinand-Nogaret (1985)

(iii) With so many bourgeois behaving like nobles and so many nobles behaving like bourgeois, it is difficult to find much evidence of class conflict between the two. Indeed it is difficult to identify them as classes at all, whether one adopts a Marxist definition of class based on economic function, or a more general definition such as that proposed by Marc Bloch, who wrote that we should consider people to be of the same class 'whose ways of life were sufficiently similar and whose material circumstances were sufficiently close not to create any conflict of interest'[1] ...

It is necessary to look at what the Revolution actually did. As soon as one does, one cannot help but be struck by the extent to which it favoured the bourgeois. At both a national and a local level it was they who benefited most from the new political arrangements ... It was not a fixed group, of course. On the contrary, the new men were in turn replaced by newer men, with the result that a large number acquired some kind of direct political experience in the course of the 1790s.

This new political class can be defined as 'bourgeois' in a loosely Marxist sense, both in terms of social position and class consciousness. Although various in terms of economic function, its members did own the means of production, whether in the form of capital, skill, tools or land. Although various in terms of political opinion, its members did unite in their rejection of feudalism, aristocracy and absolutism. Unfortunately, to use 'bourgeois' in this way does not take us very far. Such a capacious category cannot distinguish between militant republicans and moderate royalists. Neither can it accommodate the awkward fact that the most advanced parts of France, economically speaking, were often right-wing, while radical republicanism was most intense in the least capitalist regions.

Note 1. From 'Nobles, Privileges and Taxes in France at the End of the Ancien Régime', in the *Economic History Review*, xv, 1962-63

from *The French Revolution: Aristocrats Versus Bourgeois* by T.C.W. Blanning (1987)

# Q*uestions*

**1** What elements in the cartoon give Source B(iii) its satirical edge?

**(4 marks)**

**2** 'Sources A and B show how flimsy were the arguments in defence of the nobility.' Do you agree? **(8 marks)**

**3** Why, in Source C, is George Rudé so dismissive of the 'conspiracy' theory? **(5 marks)**

**4** 'Between the nobles and the bourgeois it is difficult to find much evidence of class conflict' (Source D(iii)). How far do these sources support this view? **(8 marks)**

**5** Do you agree with Blanning, (Source D(iii)), that the bourgeois were the main beneficiaries of the French Revolution? Use both the sources and your own knowledge to develop your answers.**(10 marks)**

# 4 A MIDDLE-CLASS REVOLUTION IN PARIS, 1789-91?

The middle classes helped to a very large extent to bring about a revolution in France in 1789. The growth of the capitalist economy in France in the eighteenth century, the rising expectations of the industrial, mercantile and financial classes, the ambitions of middle-class professional groups such as lawyers, publishers and of academics and intellectuals, largely shaped the agitation which developed against the ancien régime. Dissatisfaction percolated down to schoolmasters, shopkeepers and clerks in the towns, and ultimately to the mass of the illiterate peasantry in the countryside. So it was that the lower orders, all of whom had grievances of their own, came to share the grievances of their social betters. All of them scented the possibility of something better in the future, and threw in their lot with the would-be reformers.

Of course, the term 'middle class', like the Marxist term 'bourgeois', covered a very wide spectrum of society. At the top end were merchants, bankers, tax-farmers and richer professionals whose income was very large and whose possessions were vast; They had long been demanding a share of political power commensurate with their social status, and were at a loss to understand why they were denied access to the charmed circle of France's rulers. At the other end there were large numbers of minor functionaries, legal clerks, lesser professional people like teachers and journalists - even the superior sort of artisan - who claimed to be a bit better than their fellows and who demanded improvements. The broad distinction here was between those who had some social pretensions and wore breeches (culottes), and those who went to work in overalls and trousers, the 'genuine' working class. The term 'sans-culottes', however, originally referring to this latter group, came to have an important ideological significance at the time of the Terror.

In the drawing-up of the cahiers, at the time of the elections to the Estate General, and in the months after its meeting in May 1789, middle-class influences in the Revolution were almost unchallenged, though the deteriorating economic situation in Paris might have given some of the more thoughtful leaders a reason to pause. But after July 1789 cracks began to appear in the alliance. Peasants in the countryside began to take the initiative; in Paris, too, there was turbulence in the streets, and in July the Bastille was taken. This led the middle class to fear for the security of its property, and in its turn this fear led to the formation of the National Guard. Those who feared that the Revolution would unleash forces which no one would be able to control were increasingly shown to be right.

Of course, the middle classes had by no means finished their work. Many of the later acts of the National Assembly, or Constituent Assembly, as it now began to call itself, still bear the unmistakable imprint of their bourgeois origin.

## A  A Constitutional Revolution?

(i) The name NATIONAL ASSEMBLY is the only one fitting for the Assembly under present circumstances; because the members who compose it are the only ones lawfully and publicly known and verified; because they are sent directly by almost the whole nation; and because, lastly, representation being one and indivisible, none of the deputies, from whatever class or order he may be chosen has the right to perform his duties outside the present assembly...

The National Assembly orders that the motives for the present decision be drawn up immediately, to be presented to the King and to the Nation.

First Declaration of the National Assembly, 17 June 1789

(ii) The National Assembly, considering that it has been summoned to establish the constitution of the kingdom, to effect the regeneration of public order, and to maintain the true principles of monarchy; that nothing can prevent it from continuing its deliberations in whatever place it may be forced to establish itself; and, finally, that wheresoever its members are assembled, there is the National Assembly;

Decrees that all members of this assembly shall immediately take a solemn oath not to separate, and to reassemble wherever circumstances require, until the constitution of the kingdom is established upon firm foundations; and that, the said oath being taken, all members and each one individually shall ratify this steadfast resolution by signature.

Tennis Court Oath, 20 June 1789

## B  The King's Response

(i) The King wishes that the ancient distinction between the three Orders of the State should be preserved in its entirety, as essentially linked to the Constitution of this Kingdom; that the Deputies, freely elected by each of the three Orders, forming three Chambers, deliberating by Order... can alone be considered as forming the body of the representatives of this Nation. As a result, the King has declared null the resolutions passed by the deputies of the third Estate on the 17th of this month, and all subsequent ones, as illegal and unconstitutional.

Declaration of the King at the Royal Session of the Estates General, 23 June 1789

(ii) Entirely occupied in upholding the well-being of my Kingdom, and desiring above all that the assembly of the Estates General should occupy itself with matters concerning the whole nation, after the voluntary acceptance that your Order has given to my declaration of 23rd of this month, I desire my faithful nobility to unite without delay with the other two Orders to hasten the accomplishment of my paternal intentions.

Message of Louis XVI to the President of the Chamber of the Nobility, 27 June 1789

## C The National Assembly Outlines a Programme
(i) 1 The National Assembly abolishes the feudal régime entirely, and decrees that all rights and dues, both feudal and provincial, and all dues deriving from mortmain, real or personal, and personal servitude are abolished without compensation; but that all other dues are redeemable....

4 All seigneurial courts are suppressed without any indemnity....

5 Tithes of every kind, and dues that take the place of them... are abolished.

The *August Decrees* of the National Assembly, 4-11 August 1789

(ii) The representatives of the people of France, formed into a National Assembly, considering that ignorance, neglect or contempt of human rights are the sole causes of public misfortunes and corruption of governments, have resolved to set forth in a solemn declaration, those natural, inalienable and sacred rights of man; that this declaration being constantly present before the members of the social body, they may be ever kept attentive to their rights and duties; that the acts of the legislative and executive powers of the government, being capable of being directed by simple and uncontestable principles, may always tend to the maintenance of the constitution, and to the general happiness. Accordingly the National Assembly recognizes and proclaims... the following rights of man and of the citizen....

Declaration of the Rights of Man and of the Citizen, 27 August 1789

(iii)1 All powers emanate essentially from the nation and may emanate only therefrom.

2 The French government is monarchical; there is no authority in France superior to the law; the King reigns only through law, and requires obedience only in the name of law.

4 The National Assembly is permanent.

5 The National Assembly shall be composed of a single chamber.

6 Every legislature shall be of two years' duration.

9 No act of the legislative body shall be regarded as law if it is not made by the freely elected representatives of the nation, and sanctioned by the monarch.

10 In case the King refuses his consent, such refusal shall only be suspensive.

*Decree* on the Fundamental Principles of Government, 1 October 1789

(iv)1 All citizens who have the right to vote shall assemble, not in parish or community assemblies, but in primary assemblies according to cantons.
2   The active citizens, that is to say those possessing the qualifications hereinafter specified, alone shall have the right to vote, and to take part in primary assemblies in the cantons.
3   The qualifications necessary for active citizenship are: 1st, to be a native or naturalised Frenchman; 2nd, to be over 25 years of age; 3rd, to be actually domiciled in the canton for at least a year; 4th, to pay a direct tax equal to the local value of three days' labour; 5th, not to be in a position of domesticity, that is to say of a hired servant.

*Decree* Establishing Electoral Assemblies, 22 December 1789

**D   The Fall of the Bastille, 14 July 1789**
*14 July 1789.* We ran to the end of the Rue St Honoré. Here we soon perceived an immense crowd proceeding towards the Palais Royal, with acceleration of an extraordinary kind, but which sufficiently indicated a joyful event, and, as it approached, we saw a flag, some large keys, and a paper elevated on a pole above the crowd on which was inscribed 'The Bastille is taken and the gates are open'. The intelligence of this extraordinary event, thus communicated, produced an impression really indescribable. A sudden burst of frantic joy took place; every possible mode in which the most rapturous joy could be expressed, was everywhere exhibited. Shouts and shrieks, leaping and embracing, laughter and tears... manifested, among the promiscuous crowd, such a unanimous emotion of extreme gladness as I should suppose was never before experienced by human beings.

from *Letters from France in 1789* by Edward Rigby, ed. Lady Eastlake (1880)

**E   The October Days, 1789**
Versailles, 9 October 1789. We have had dreadful doings. On the 6th, at night, a set of wretches forced themselves into the palace, screaming: *'The head of the Queen! Down with the Queen! No more Louis as King; we want the Duke of Orleans! He'll let us have bread!'.*
M. Durepaire, one of the Queen's bodyguard, defended the Queen's door and was killed. Mme. Thibaud woke the Queen, who threw a coverlet from the bed over her and ran to the King's room; and soon after she had gone, her door was burst open. The King ran to fetch his son, and all together they waited the event. They owed their rescue to M. Lafayette and the French Guard. He insisted on the King

taking up his abode in Paris, without which he would not promise him safety. At one the next day, therefore, they all went, partly escorted by the fishwives and their bullies. They were six hours travelling from Versailles to Paris.

*from a letter of Mrs Henry Swinburne to her husband, October 1789*

**F   The Massacre of the Champ de Mars, 17 July 1791**
(i) All sections of the Realm demand that Louis be tried! You, Gentlemen, have judged in advance that he was innocent.... Legislators, this was not the will of the people; and we had thought that your greatest glory - even your duty - consisted in being the agents of the public will. Without doubt, gentlemen, you have been won over to this decision by refractory deputies.... Everything dictates that we demand that you, in the name of all France... receive his abdication, convoke a new constituent power to proceed in a truly national manner to try the culprit, and, above all, to replace him and his organisation by a new executive power.

*Second Petition* from radical agitators assembled on the Champ de Mars, 17 July 1791

(ii) The radicals were appalled when the King was not put on trial. Their anger was directed against the Assembly, which they claimed no longer represented the people...

   On 17 July 1791, 50 000 people flocked to the Champ de Mars, a huge field where the Feast of the Federation, celebrating the Fall of the Bastille, had been held three days earlier. They were there to sign a republican petition on the 'altar of the Fatherland'. This was a political demonstration of the poorer sections of the Paris population. The Commune, under pressure from the Assembly, declared martial law. They sent Lafayette with the National Guard to the Champ de Mars, where the Guard fired on the peaceful and unarmed crowd. About 50 people were killed.

   This was the first bloody clash between different groups in the Third Estate, and it was greeted with pleasure in the Assembly.

*from France in Revolution by Duncan Townson (1990)*

**G   A Parisian Revolution**
(i) Up to this point [the dismissal of Necker, 11 July 1789] the Revolution had been a matter of laws: now it came down to street level. The most important incident was the storming of the Bastille, on 14 July 1789. Did this mean it was a Parisian Revolution? No doubt: but it was followed, and in some cases, preceded, by a whole series of revolts in towns throughout France. Was it a popular Revolution? Certainly: the emergence of the urban masses was the most significant aspect of these events. However, it was also a bourgeois

Revolution, the revolt of a bourgeoisie which was still very far from having achieved its aims, and which was therefore not yet reluctant to become involved.

from *The Fall of the French Monarchy, 1787-92* by Michel Vovelle (1972)

(ii) From the beginning of the Revolution, serious contradictions began to emerge between the rhetoric of liberty, equality and fraternity and the reality of a revolution led by a wealthy, propertied élite. It was one thing for noble and clerical deputies on 4 August, intoxicated by the revolutionary movement, to declare that the feudal régime was 'abolished in its entirety', quite another for the land-owning deputies, in the sober light of day, to agree to the end of all seigneurial payments. Abolition of church tithe and personal dues smacking of the feudal past, yes, but seigneurial dues relating to land contracts, definitely not. 'PROPERTY' is the key word which unlocks the major mysteries of the Revolution. Although the Declaration of the Rights of Man begins with the famous formulation that 'all men are born free and equal in rights', we have to recall that Article 17 declared property to be 'inviolable and sacred'. Edmund Burke, in his famous work *Reflections on the French Revolution,* spotted the main contradiction which was to be the curse of the Revolution - the incompatibility of general, universal, or what Burke called 'metaphysical' truths with the very particular, individual property rights of the ruling élite.

from *The French Revolution: Rethinking the Debate* by Gwynne Lewis (1993)

# Questions

1 How convincingly does the Tiers Etat justify the exceeding of its legal powers in Sources A(i) and A(ii)? **(6 marks)**

2 In the light of his statements made in Sources B(i) and B(ii), what criticisms can be made of the King's leadership during the early stages of the Revolution? **(8 marks)**

3 Using the sources and your own knowledge, assess how far the changes in Source C represented a 'revolution'.(10 marks)

4 'Source D is more useful to the historian than Source E.' To what extent do you agree? **(6 marks)**

5 Does the evidence in Sources A-F give greater support to the views expressed in Source G(i) or to those of Source G(ii)? Explain your answer. **(10 marks)**

(see Page 101 for a specimen source-based question answer.)

# 5 PARIS AND THE PROVINCES: THE GREAT FEAR

The Revolution in Paris and in a number of the larger municipalities in provincial France in the summer of 1789 was paralleled by serious disturbances in the countryside. The background to these was the development of capitalistic, in place of traditional, agricultural methods and the tightening noose of feudal reaction as aristocrats sought to augment their incomes by reviving obsolete obligations and by introducing new and cost-efficient methods of managing their estates. But it was harvest failures and actual food shortages on the eve of the revolution which made things really critical. There were unco-ordinated attacks on noble property during the summer, a number of which showed evidence of the peasants' desire to withhold the services traditionally performed for their lords; local aristocrats found these so-called *jacqueries* extremely alarming. It was only the intervention of the new bourgeoisie that had just assumed power that put a check to them.

These rural revolts led up to and helped to explain what became later known as the 'Great Fear'. Rumours began to spread at the end of July that bands of armed brigands and mercenaries were on their way, looting and destroying so as to avenge events in Paris and reassert the pretensions of the monarchy and the nobility. Traditional enemies of France were supposed to be marching with the brigands, as were a variety of ex-convicts and escapees from the prison-hulks. Massacres, battles and atrocities were rumoured, and there was a rush to arms. It is true that begging gangs and workless vagrants were on the move as the result of the famine, but generally there was no cause for panic and most of the rumours in the end proved to be baseless.

There followed a second phase, when the villagers did not lay down their arms, but moved to form their local equivalents of the Parisian National Guard. They also embarked on their own revolution at the village level. Title deeds, land registers, feudal documents and the like were confiscated and destroyed; after the Decrees of August, the attack on feudalism, legalised in Paris, moved systematically forward. There were outrages and casualties, but the stories grew as they were repeated, and by the end of the year most had blown over. None the less, the geographical course of the Great Fear can be plotted on the map, and most of the provinces - except Alsace-Lorraine, Brittany, Languedoc and lower Provence - experienced it. The problem involved the destruction of the old social framework and the hierarchy of orders; for when feudalism had been destroyed other structures had to be devised to take its place.

## A   The Masses in Paris

(i) *26 August:* I have already demanded that attention be devoted to
provisioning Paris with grain... I saw that the grain bought by the
government is running out... and that it was necessary to have a
stockpile of food in reserve, to prevent any cause, or pretext, for an
insurrection and that such a stockpile could only be obtained abroad...
The cartloads of flour in our convoys are not only pillaged on the way
by mobs, but are also pillaged in Paris by bakers who wait for them
in the suburbs... Such disorder creates two serious problems: the first
is that the distribution of flour is unequal; one baker has too much,
another not enough; the second is that the Paris market is poorly
stocked, which upsets public opinion.

from *Mémoirs of Bailly,* first President of the National Assembly (1789)

(ii) How will it all end? This unhappy country presents to one's moral
view a mighty ruin. Like the remnants of ancient magnificence, we
admire the architecture of the temple, while we detest the false god to
whom it was dedicated. Daws and ravens and birds of night now
build their nests in its niches; the sovereign, humbled to the level of a
beggar's pity, without resources, without authority, without a friend;
the Assembly, at once a master and a slave - new in power, wild in
theory, raw in practice, it engrosses all functions, though incapable of
exercising any, and has taken from this fierce, ferocious people every
restraint of religion and respect.

from the *Diary* of Gouverneur Morris, 19 November 1790

## B   The Results of Bread Shortages

(i) The inhabitants of the parish of Lugny-Champagne are complaining
that at the beginning of the harvest time there arrived in the district a
huge number of male and female gleaners from other areas who
flooded into the fields that were still piled with sheaves and spread
themselves everywhere; the men in charge of the fields could not get
them out; not only did they glean among the sheaves, but if the
farmer tried to say anything, they poured abuse on him; they even
chased away the poor from the village itself. To guard against such
inconvenience, the inhabitants want no itinerants to be allowed to
glean... and as for those who are not travellers, they must only be
permitted to glean if they have a certificate of good character signed
by their priest.

from the *Cahier* of Lugny-Champagne (Bailliwick of Bourges), 1789,
reprinted in *Frenchmen Speak, 1789,* eds. P. Goubert & M. Denis (1964)

(ii) Being here on a market day at Nangis [south-east of Paris], I
attended and saw the wheat sold out, with a party of dragoons drawn
up before the market-cross to prevent violence. The people quarrel

with the bakers, asserting the prices they demand for bread are out of all proportion with the wheat, and proceeding from words to scuffling, raise riot, and then run away with the wheat and the bread for nothing. This has happened at many other markets; the consequence was that neither farmers nor bakers would supply them till they were in danger of starving, and, when they did come, prices rose enormously, which aggravated the mischief, till troops became really necessary to give security to those who supplied the markets.

from *Travels in France* by Arthur Young (1788-9)

### C  The Great Fear in the Provinces

(i) On 27 July 1789, a party of unknown brigands, together with my own vassals and those of a neighbouring parish to mine, came, to the number of two hundred, to my castle of Sassy, near to Argentan, and, after breaking the locks of the closets which held my title-deeds, took from them a large collection together with the registers which are essential for me, and took them away and burnt them in the woods near my castle; my guard could not make any resistance, since he was alone in looking after this estate, where I do not reside. The wretches rang the alarm-bell in neighbouring parishes to gather to their support a greater number. I am indeed most unfortunate in this loss because I have never imposed on my vassals the hateful burdens of traditional feudalism, from which I agree they should be freed in present circumstances; but who can assess and prove the damage they have done to my property?

from the *Appeal* of the Count de Germiny to the National Assembly, August 1789

(ii) There is daily talk of attacking the nobility, or setting fire to their castles in order to burn all their title-deeds... In those cantons where unrest has been less sensational, the inhabitants meet daily to pass resolutions that they will pay no more rent or other seigneurial dues, but fix a moderate price for the redemption of these, and lower the rate of dues; endless hostile projects of this sort spring from that spirit of equality and independence which prevails in men's minds today.

Statement by M. d'Ornacieux, President of the Barony of Thodure, 28 June 1789

(iii) When the inhabitants of Saint-Genest saw this great crowd of men passing by in some disorder and carrying arms, they became much afraid and shouted to Batigne's son from La Poussié who was working in the fields, telling him to hurry to Réalmont and say that some rebel fanatics had come and burnt down the church at Sainy-Genest. It was between six and seven in the evening, and this boy caused such a panic and confusion that everybody came out armed with halberds, pikes, pitchforks and so on; they joined the militia in the market place; the consuls had logs piled up at the gates to stop anyone coming in; but nobody came.

from Account of Camisard[1] troubles near Castres, 22 September 1789

Note 1. Religious riots between the Catholic population and armed local Protestants.

(v)

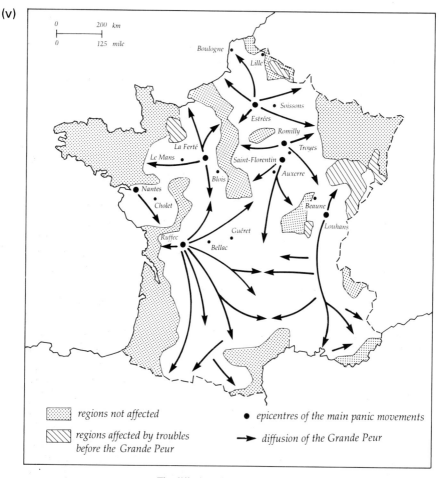

The diffusion of the Grande Peur

## D Disturbances in Provincial Towns

*21 July 1789:* Passing through the square of the City Hall [in Strasburg], the mob were breaking the windows with stones, although an officer and a detachment of horse were in the square... Perceiving that the troops would not attack them, except in words, they grew more violent, and furiously attempted to beat the doors in pieces with iron crowbars, placing ladders to the windows. In about a quarter of an hour, which gave time for the assembled magistrates to escape by a back door, they burst all open, and entered like a torrent with a universal shout of the spectators. From that moment, a shower of casements, sashes, shutters, chairs, tables, sofas, books, pictures, papers etc. rained incessantly from all the windows of the house, which is 70 or 80 feet long, and which was succeeded by tiles, skirting-boards and every part of the building that force could detach... I remarked several common soldiers with their white cockades among the plunderers, instigating the mob even in the sight of their officers. There were amongst them people so decently dressed that I regarded them with no small surprise; they destroyed all the public archives; the streets for some way round strewed with papers. This had become a wanton mischief.

from *Travels in France* by Arthur Young (1788-9)

**E   Later Views of the Great Fear**
(i) Under the *ancien régime,* begging was one of the scourges of the countryside; from 1787 onwards unemployment and rising prices made it worse... Every beggar, vagrant and rioter seemed to be a 'brigand'. There had always been great anxiety at harvest time: it was a moment the peasants dreaded; local alarms increased daily...

There is no trace of plot or conspiracy at the start of the Great Fear. It was far from foolish to fear the vagrant, but the aristocrat-brigand was a phantom figure. The revolutionaries helped to spread his image, but they acted in good faith. If they spread the rumour of the aristocrats' plot it was because they believed it. They exaggerated its importance out of all proportion: only the court considered using force against the Third Estate, and they showed themselves pathetically incompetent in its execution. The men of the revolution did not make the mistake of despising their adversaries, and they were inclined to fear the worst. Furthermore, they did not need the Great Fear to bring the towns in on their side; the municipal revolution had already taken place and this was a decisive point in their favour. As for the unfortunate poor who constantly moaned and murmured behind the bourgeoisie in both town and country, they gave great cause for concern; the bourgeoisie had everything to fear from their outbursts of despair. It was natural for the enemies of revolution to accuse its supporters of encouraging the poor to overthrow the ancien régime so that they could put in its place a new order where the new men could rule - but it was equally natural for the revolutionaries to suspect the aristocracy of fomenting anarchy to keep them out of power.

from *The Great Fear of 1789* by Georges Lefebvre (1933)

(ii) It has become commonplace to talk about the 'revolutions' of the summer of 1789 in the plural. This is no doubt a salutary reaction against the artifical unanimity of a certain old-fashioned interpretation which was simplistic and did not go into detail. According to Mathiez, there was first a Paris revolution, then a revolution in the provinces which gained urban support, and then finally a revolution in the countryside. According to Lefebvre, the phases were not geographical but social: the process began with an aristocratic revolution and moved on through a bourgeois revolution, to a revolution of the people, and finally to a revolution of the peasants. This scheme was more or less adopted by Soboul. All these schemes are certainly useful pedagogically but, more important, they take into account the genuinely diverse strands of a revolution which was not monolithic. The reactions of the bourgeoisie to the Great Fear indicate that the revolt of the peasants was an autonomous movement; on the other hand, the bourgeois militia offers us the spectacle of an armed bourgeoisie opposed both to absolutism and to the dangers of a popular explosion.

from *The Fall of the French Monarchy, 1787-92* by Michel Vovelle (1972)

# Questions

1 What can be deduced from Sources A and B about the reasons for lawlessness in the early years of the Revolution?  **(6 marks)**

2 Using your own knowledge, comment on the validity of Gouverneur Morris's view of the Revolution (Source A(ii)) at the end of 1790.
  **(6 marks)**

3 (a) How does Source C explain the rapid spread of the Great Fear?
  (b) What are the uses and limitations of this map as historical evidence?  **(4 + 4 marks)**

4 'The aristocrat-brigand was a phantom figure' (Source E(i)). Is this view supported by the evidence in Sources C and D?  **(6 marks)**

5 What support for Vovelle's views on the bourgeoisie (final sentence of Source E(ii)) can be found in Sources C and D?  **(6 marks)**

6 What difficulties face any historian attempting to write an objective assessment of the Great Fear?  **(8 marks)**

# 6 THE ATTACK ON THE CHURCH
## AND THE FALL OF THE MONARCHY

The attack on the Catholic Church in France sought to deprive it of its
privileges in French society. It was part of the great levelling that
followed the Declaration of the Rights of Man. It also provided the
government with a chance to solve another problem - that of state
bankruptcy. An effort was made to re-establish public credit on the basis
of the lands taken from the Church. These assets could not all be
realised at once without knocking the bottom out of the land market;
none the less, they could be valued and bonds could be issued against
their supposed value. These bonds were the assignats, controlled by a
special bank set up for the purpose. The assignats soon became legal
tender, and their systematic over-issue created the high level of inflation
which was one of the main features of the Revolution.

In 1790 there followed a more comprehensive reform, the *Civil
Constitution of the Clergy*. It had never been the government's aim to bring
about changes in religious dogma; nor was there any intention to
separate church and state. But the new law achieved four main
objectives: it changed ecclesiastical boundaries to fit the new local
government, making the boundaries of dioceses identical with those of
the new departments; it provided for the election of priests and other
ecclesiastical officials; it decreed that in future French clerics should
receive state salaries; and it effectively severed the links which bound the
church to the Papacy.

Understandably, such measures were denounced by Pope Pius VI. In
November, therefore, the Assembly imposed on all clergy a *Clerical Oath*,
requiring them to uphold the provisions of the Civil Constitution. This
split in the ranks of the clergy between the 'constitutional' clergy and the
'non-juring' (or 'refractory') clergy. The Pope issued a Bull condemning
the changes, and the French government then broke off relations with
Rome in May 1791.

All this was very disturbing to Louis XVI. A man of simple piety, he
could not bring himself to give his assent to the new laws, especially
when the Pope condemned them. He was persuaded by the Queen to
flee to the eastern frontier, where his brother sovereigns would gather
an army with a view to restoring him. But everything went wrong. The
royal refugees, travelling slowly in a comfortable coach instead of
rapidly in a fast one, were ignominiously arrested at Varennes and
brought back to Paris almost as prisoners. The French government
strongly denounced his actions and threatened him with deposition

if anything similar occurred in future.

War against Austria, whose Emperor was the Queen's brother, and Prussia soon after (April 1792) further undermined the King's position. There followed two attacks upon the Tuileries Palace: one in June, when the King and the Royal Family were endangered and humiliated, the second on 10 August, after which he and his family fled to the Assembly for protection. They were imprisoned in the Temple for their own safety. Shortly after, the Legislative Assembly and the 1791 Constitution on which it was based, collapsed. A National Convention was hastily elected in September, and one of the first things it did was to declare a republic and bring the King to trial. Moderates argued that Louis had been sufficiently punished by being removed from his throne, but Jacobin leaders in the Convention were not so easily satisfied and insisted on further vengeance. In December he was arraigned and brought to trial, and in January he was guillotined. During his trial and at his execution he bore himself with dignity and patience, and his death shocked not only the majority of Frenchmen, but almost the whole of European opinion as well. His queen, Marie Antoinette, followed him to the guillotine on 17 October 1793.

## A  The Fate of the Church Estates
(i) 1. The National Assembly declares that all ecclesiastical property is at the disposal of the state for the purpose of providing in a suitable manner for the conduct of worship, the maintenance of the clergy and the relief of the poor.

*Declaration* of the National Assembly, 2 November 1789

(ii) 1. The debts of the clergy are considered as national debts; the public treasury shall be responsible for paying their interest and principal. The nation declares that whosoever holds contracts of revenues assigned to the clergy are considered creditors of the state. Accordingly, the nation appropriates and mortgages to them all property and revenues at its disposal... 3. The assignats created by decree and sanctioned by the King shall be legal tender throughout the kingdom, and shall be received as coin of the realm.

*Decree* on Assignats, 17 April 1790

## B  The Civil Constitution of the Clergy
*Title I : Of Ecclesiastical Offices*
1. Each department shall constitute a single diocese, and each diocese shall have the same extent and limits as the department.
*Title II : Of Appointment to Benefices*
1. Dating from the date of the present decree, appointments to bishoprics and curés are to be made by election only. 16. Not later than a month after his election, the bishop-elect shall present himself

to his metropolitan bishop... and shall request him to grant canonical confirmation. 19. The new bishop may not apply to the Pope for confirmation of his election; but he shall write to him as visible Head of the universal church in testimony of the unity of the faith.

*Title III : Of the Salaries of Ministers of Religion*
1. Ministers of religion, performing the most important functions of society, and obliged to reside continuously in their place of service, shall be maintained by the nation.

*Title IV : Of the Law of Residence*
1. The law of residence shall be strictly observed, and all who are invested with ecclesiastical office shall be subject thereto without distinction or exception.

from Civil Constitution of the Clergy, 12 July 1790

**C  The Clerical Oath**
1. Bishops, archbishops and priests maintained in office shall be required to take an oath... concerning the Civil Constitution of the Clergy. Accordingly they shall swear to watch carefully over the faithful of the diocese or parish entrusted to them, to be faithful to the nation, to the law and to the King, and to maintain with all their power the Constitution decreed by the National Assembly... 5. Those who have not, within the prescribed periods, taken the oath prescribed for them, shall be deemed to have renounced their office.

Decree Requiring a Clerical Oath, 27 November 1790

**D  The Flight to Varennes, June 1791**
(i) The outrages committed upon and the threats made against my family and myself were the reasons for my departure. Since that time, several writings have sought to provoke violence against myself and my family, and so far these insults have gone unpunished. Thenceforth I felt that I lacked security and even decency so long as I remained in Paris.

Accordingly I wished to leave that city. Being unable to do so publicly, I resolved to leave at night and unattended. I never intended to leave the kingdom; I had no agreement in that connection with either foreign powers or my relatives.

Declaration by King Louis XVI, 27 June 1791

(ii) We will content ourselves with saying that, surrounded by a barrier of five hundred thousand citizens, of whom many were armed, Louis XVI, his wife and his sister arrived at the Tuileries between seven and half-past. No sign of disapproval, no apparent sign of contempt escaped from the numerous gathering. It was confined to denying any military honours to these fugitives. They were received with grounded arms. All the citizens kept their hats on as if in common agreement.

from Article in *Courier of the 83 Departments,* June 1791

(iii) 1. If the King, after taking his oath to the Constitution, retracts it, he shall be deemed to have abdicated. 2. If the King places himself at the head of an army to direct forces against the nation, or if he does not oppose by formal statement every act of such type executed in his name, he shall be deemed to have abdicated.

Decree Defining Abdication, 16 July 1791

### E   The Attack on the Tuileries, 10 August 1792

(i) 22 June 1792. The attempt of the Jacobins to intimidate His Most Christian Majesty has failed entirely and has served to impress on the minds of those who wish for good government an abhorrence of their principles. The majesty of the throne was sullied, but it gave the King the opportunity of displaying an extraordinary degree of calmness and courage, which may be of infinite service...

The King, finding the mob determined to force the door of the antechamber of his apartment, ordered his attendants to withdraw and placed himself in the recess of one of the windows, where he suffered the mob to approach him, accepted from them a red cap with tricolour ribbons which he wore whilst they were in the palace, and, upon their expressing a wish that he should drink to the health of the nation, His Majesty complied with their request and drank the remains of some wine in a cup, from which a grenadier had previously drunk.

Dispatches of Earl Gower, British Ambassador to Paris, ed. O. Browning (1885)

(ii) On 10 August the inhabitants of all the suburbs went to the Tuileries Palace, accompanied by all the Sections of Paris, armed in the same manner as they were on 20 June, and calling for the dethronement of the King - that he was a traitor and had forfeited the throne... The Palace of the Tuileries is now almost wholly destroyed, the doors and windows of it being broken to pieces... During all these disorders, the King and the royal family were sitting in the National Assembly, where they had taken refuge... The sansculottes have now achieved all their ends.

from *The Times,* 16 August 1792

### F   The Trial and Execution of the King, December 1792-January 1793

(i) *3 December 1792:* For myself I abhor the death penalty freely imposed by your laws, and I have neither love nor hatred for Louis; I hate only crime. I demanded the abolition of the death penalty from the Assembly, and it is not my fault if the first principle of reason seemed to them heresy. But if you never sought to invoke it in favour of so many unhappy people whose crimes are less, why do you remember it now to plead the cause of the greatest of all criminals? You ask for an exception to the death penalty for him alone who would make it legitimate!... Now, public safety never required the death penalty for ordinary crimes, because society can always prevent them by other means, and render the culprit incapable of doing further harm. But a king... whose very name draws the scourge of war on a nation in tumult, neither prison nor exile can make his existence indifferent to the public welfare; and this cruel exception can be imputed only to the nature of his crimes. I pronounce with regret this fatal truth - that Louis must die because the motherland must live!

*Speech* by Maximilien Robespierre in the Debate in the National Convention about the Trial of the King

(ii) Louis mounted the throne at the age of twenty, and even then he set an example of morality; he was governed by no culpable weaknesses, no corrupting passion; he was economical, just and severe and proved himself a friend of his country. The nation desired the abolition of crushing tax; he revoked it. The people demanded the abolition of servitude; he abolished it in his domains. They prayed for reforms in the criminal law; he made those reforms. They demanded that thousands of Frenchmen excluded from political rights should acquire and enjoy them; he conceded them. The people demanded liberty; he gave it. He even anticipated their wishes by his sacrifices; yet it is in the name of this same people that men are now demand-ing - Citizens, I shall not continue. I pause before the tribunal of history. Remember that it will judge your decision, and your decision will be the voice of ages.

*Speech* for the Defence at the Trial of Louis XVI by Romain Desèze, 26 December 1792

(iii) Citizens, the tyrant is no more! For a long time, the cries of the victims, whom war and domestic strife have spread over France and Europe, loudly protested his existence. He has paid his penalty, and only acclamations for the Republic and for liberty have been heard from the people...

The National Convention and the French people now have only one mind and only one sentiment, that of liberty and civic fraternity.

Now, above all, we need peace in the interior of the Republic, and the most active watch on the domestic enemies of liberty. Never did circumstances more urgently required the sacrifice of their passions and their personal opinions concerning the act of national justice which has just been carried out. Today the French people have no other passion than that for liberty.

*Proclamation* of the National Convention to the French People, 23 January 1793

(iv)  Execution  of  King  Louis  XIV,  21  January  1793

# Q u e s t i o n s

1 'The church reforms of 1790 were merely an attempt to tackle clerical abuses.' To what extent does the evidence of Sources A-C support this view? **(6 marks)**

2 'Louis XVI lacked political judgment and skill, but he did not lack personal courage.' Is this view supported by Sources D and E? **(5 marks)**

3 'Robespierre appealed to reason, Desèze to the emotions.' How far do you agree with this comparison of Sources F(i) and F(ii)? **(6 marks)**

4 How far is Source F(iii) an attempt to justify the execution of the King? **(5 marks)**

5 Do Sources D-F show that the King's fate was inevitable? **(8 marks)**

6 Use all the sources in this Unit, and your own knowledge, to show that the fates of the French church and monarchy were closely bound up together. **(10 marks)**

# 7 WHO WERE THE MOB?

The Paris 'mob' is reckoned to have played a major role in the Revolution, especially during the period known as the 'Terror'. Though they were often dismissed as scum or 'dog-stuff' *(canaille)*, it seems likely that the true composition of the mob was more socially mixed and altogether more respectable.

They were perhaps freakish in appearance. Many of them cultivated extravagant moustaches, with bushy sideburns and long, unkempt locks (though full beards at the time were not quite as fashionable); they wore revolutionary rosettes and various other favours, carried a variety of weapons and generally behaved in a wild and threatening fashion. But most were solidly working class, with a good sprinkling of those who were socially much better than they pretended to be - small employers, journalists, junior civil servants, clerks, shop-keepers, and even a few wine-merchants and wholesalers. Though some of them still continued to wear the breeches of the upper and middle classes, most of them wore the trousers of the labouring class - hence the name of *sans-culotte*. There was an inverted snobbery about being a *sans-culotte:* many individuals of quite substantial means affected their style of dress and behaviour; some, even, were propertied people. The genuine sans-culotte lived in rented apartments on the fourth or fifth floor, where, on account of all the stairs to be climbed, rents were lower than they were for the lower floors. Many participated actively in the affairs of the local Jacobin Club in their *Section* of the city.

The most wildly radical sans-culottist leaders were known as 'mad dogs' *(enragés)* and adopted extremist views such as those of Jacques Roux, a former priest who advocated pensions for supporters and death for opponents, and of Jacques René Hébert, who eventually succeeded in achieving his aim of abolishing the French church. A handful, in their programme of ruthless price controls, a lower *Maximum* for bread and municipal stores to sell goods at rock-bottom prices, anticipated the later socialist thinking of François Noel ('Gracchus') Babeuf. So extreme and impractical were the views of the *enragés* that they antagonised the mainstream Jacobins such as Robespierre and his colleagues in the Committee of Public Safety; and early in 1794 many of them were purged. A number of them were women activists, and they shared in the general eclipse of the *enragés* at this time.

## A The Views of the Sans-culottes

(i) What is a sans-culotte, you rogues? He is someone who always goes about on foot, who has not got the millions you would all like to have; who has no château, no valets to wait on him, and who lives simply with his wife and children, if he has any, on the fourth or fifth floor. If you wish to meet the cream of sans-culotterie, then visit the garrets of the working-men. The sans-culotte is useful because he knows how to plough a field, to forge iron, use a saw, to file, to roof a house, to make shoes - and to spill his blood to the last drop for the safety of the Republic. And because he is a worker, you will certainly not find him in the Café de Chartres, nor in the gaming houses where others plot and wager, nor in the National Theatre, where *L'Ami des Lois*[1] is being performed, nor in the Vaudeville Theatre at a performance of *Chaste Suzanne*[2]...

In the evening he goes to the Assembly of his Section, not powdered and perfumed and nattily booted in the hope of being noticed by the citizenesses in the gallery, but ready to give his unreserved support to sound resolutions, and ready to pulverize those which come from the despised faction of politicians.

Besides this, the sans-culotte always has his sword with the edge sharpened, ready to cut off the ears of all opponents of the Revolution. Sometimes he carries his pike with him, and at the first beat of the drum he will be seen leaving for the Vendée, for the Army of the Alps or for the Army of the North.

Notes. 1 A fashionable light comedy in Paris in 1793. 2 A popular light operetta.

A sans-culotte view of himself, from Père Duchesne, May 1793

(ii) Of course I am a Terrorist. But the only proof I have ever given of it was before the castle of the tyrant Capet on the 10 August,[1] when my terrorism cost me my right arm.

Admission by Jacques René Hébert before the Assembly of the Section des Marchés, June 1793

Note. 1 That is, in the attack on the Tuileries Palace, 1792. Capet was Louis XVI's family name, and 'Louis Capet' was an insulting way to refer to the King.

(iii)

**Republican moustaches, or good patriots. Parisians lovingly cultivated their whiskers as part of the trappings of Terror**

43

(iv) The aristocrat is a man who, because of scorn or indifference, has not been entered on the register of the National Guard and who has not taken the Civic Oath. He is a man who, by his conduct, his speeches and his writings, as well as by his connections, has given proof that he bitterly regrets the passing of the ancien régime and despises every aspect of the Revolution. He is a man whose conduct suggests that he would send cash to the *émigrés* or join the enemy army, if he had the cash to do the one or the opportunity to do the other. He is a man who has always despaired of the triumph of the Revolution, who has spread bad news which is obviously false... He is a man who has done nothing to improve the lives of the poor and who does not wear a cockade of three inches circumference; a man who buys clothes other than the national dress, and who takes no pride in the title and appearance of a sans-culotte. The true language of the Republic tells you that this definition is fair, and that the real patriot has done quite the opposite for the public well-being.

A *sans-culotte* definition of an aristocrat, May 1793

## B Who Joined the Revolutionary Mob?

It appears to have been a feature of the more organised, political movements - such as the Champ de Mars affair and the armed attacks on the Bastille and the Tuileries - that the driving element was the small shop-keepers and workshop masters, who in many cases brought their garçons, journeymen and apprentices along with them. In this connection it is perhaps of interest to note the sustained militancy of certain trades such as furnishing, building, metal-work and dress. Most conspicuous of all were the lock-smiths, joiners and cabinet-makers, shoe-makers and tailors; others frequently in evidence were stone-masons, hair-dressers and engravers; and, of those engaged in less skilful occupations, wine merchants, water-carriers, porters, cooks and domestic servants...

Even if it can be demonstrated that the majority of the participants in all... the revolutionary *journées* were Parisian sans-culottes, how far can they be considered typical of the social groups from which they were drawn? Some, while not denying the presence in the revolution- ary crowds of tradesmen, wage-earners and city poor, insisted nevertheless that the dominant element were vagabonds, criminals and unemployed. It is perhaps not surprising that such a charge should be made: it was certainly voiced on more than one occasion by hostile journalists and the police authorities. Yet, in its application to the capital at least, it has little foundation in fact... Doubtless these elements mingled with the rioters during the Revolution, but they appear to have played an altogether minor role.

This does not mean that unemployed workers or workers living in furnished rooms or lodging-houses (the *non-domiciliés*) did not form a substantial element in revolutionary crowds... In view of their numbers it is hardly surprising to find them fairly well represented among those taking part in the disturbances... but this is, of course, quite a separate question, and gives no further indication of the number of vagabonds involved.

The further contention that criminals and bandits played a significant part in the revolutionary *journées* collapses no less readily when looked at more closely... By and large it does not appear, in fact, that those taking part in revolutionary crowds were any more given to crime, or even violence and disorder, than the ordinary run of Parisian citizens from whom they were recruited.

from *The Crowd in the French Revolution* by George Rudé (1959)

**C   The *Enragés* and the Parisian Radicals.**

The aristocrat was such a figure of hatred to sans-culotterie that it was not long before the expression was being used to describe all their enemies, irrespective of whether they belonged to the former nobility or to the higher ranks of what had been the Third Estate...

The economic crisis helped to sharpen these social conflicts, and as the crisis developed differences of opinion between the sans-culottes and the upper classes of the Third Estate were added to the funda-mental sansculotte-aristocrat antagonism...An address to the Conven-tion on 27 Ventôse contrasts with the 'brave sans-culottes' not only the clergy, nobility and the crowned heads of Europe, but also the solicitors, barristers, notaries, and particularly

> well-to-do farmers, selfish citizens and all these fat, wealthy
> merchants. They are fighting against us, instead of our oppressors.

Is this simply a struggle between those who owned property and those who did not? One really cannot say that it is, for we find craftsmen and shop-keepers amongst the sans-culotterie who were themselves property-owners. It is rather a conflict between those who favoured the idea of restricted and limited ownership, and those who believed in the absolute right of property as proclaimed in 1789; and even more clearly between the defenders of a system of controls and fixed prices, and those who preferred an economic policy of *laisser-faire*...

It would appear from this that in order to gain a true picture of the sans-culotte it is necessary to depict him in opposition to the aristocracy, wealth and commerce. The need for so negative an approach shows how vague the social boundaries within the old Third Estate were, and how difficult it is to define sans-culotterie as a social class... It is these contradictions which explain its incapacity to formulate a coherent policy and, in the last analysis, its defeat.

Popular hostility against wealth and trade brought with it certain contradictions, in as much as the sans-culotte shop-keeper and craftsman often owned his own premises. Their spokesmen were always careful to explain that their anger was directed simply against property-owning on a large scale. The violent outbursts in the *Père Duchesne* arose from the fact that 'the *gros* continued to eat up the *petits*'...

Fully aware of the fundamental antagonisms of the society of the ancien régime, and consumed with hatred for the aristocracy - a hatred they shared with the radical bourgeoisie - sans-culotterie was not really 'class-conscious'. Divided into different social categories, sometimes with conflicting aims, it was practically impossible for them to constitute a class: their unity, in so far as it existed, was of a negative kind. According to popular thinking, a sans-culotte could not be defined by social characteristics alone: a counter-revolutionary workman could not be a good sans-culotte; a bourgeois patriot and republican might very well be accepted as one. *Père Duchesne* announced:

> One can only find virtue and patriotism amongst the sans-culottes; without them, the Revolution would be finished. The salvation of the Republic lies in their hands.

Here, the word sans-culotte is being used as a synonym for patriot and republican.

from *The Parisian Sans-culottes and the French Revolution* by Albert Soboul (1964)

# Questions

1 Do Sources A(i)-(iv) support the view that 'the sans-culottes' were 'consumed with hatred for the aristocracy'? Give reasons for your answer.  **(6 marks)**

2 What traditional views about the revolutionary mob is Rudé attempting to challenge in Source B?  **(6 marks)**

3 How far are Sources B and C in agreement?  **(7 marks)**

4 What, according to Sources B and C, were the aims of the sans-culottes?  **(9 marks)**

5 From your own knowledge and from the sources consider the importance of the role of the Paris mob in the Revolution.

**(12 marks)**

# 8 GIRONDINS AND JACOBINS

The outbreak of the war in April 1792, followed by the attacks on the Tuileries in June and August and the fall of the Monarchy, seriously weakened the authority of the Legislative Assembly, as did Austrian victories on the north-eastern frontier and the Prussian capture of Longwy and Verdun. Having decreed the election of a National Convention, the Assembly slipped into limbo, its authority usurped by the newly-established insurrectionary republican Commune. This initiated measures of 'public safety', closing the city gates and rounding up suspects in thousands of house-to-house searches. There followed the gruesome episode known as the 'September Massacres', when about 1400 inmates of the over-crowded Paris prisons were put to death by armed gangs, with or without the formality of a trial. By this time, elections to the Convention were already under way, and on 20 September it met.

Its sessions took place until mid-1793 in the *Manège*, or Royal Riding School. About 280 of the 749 members had earlier belonged to either the Constituent or the Legislative Assemblies. The bulk of the membership came from provincial France. There were no formal parties, but the moderates and the Right were broadly agreed on policies aimed at stable government and sound finance, their leaders including Guadet, Vergniaud and Brissot. They possessed the best orators, and the salon of Madame Roland was their intellectual headquarters. On the Left sat the Jacobins, led by Robespierre, Danton, Desmoulins and Marat. All were prominent members of the Jacobin Club, and worked closely with the local Jacobin Clubs and with the Commune, representing in general the democratic republicanism of the lower classes and the *sans-culottes*.

The central gangway did not run exactly down the middle of the hall of the *Manège*, but divided it unequally. Hence on the Left the benches were tiered up towards the roof, and so were known as the 'Mountain'; the higher the back-benchers, the wilder they usually were. Across from them, on the flat, sat the majority of the Moderates and the Right, often called the 'Plain' or more contemptuously the 'Marsh' (the *'Marais'*) by their opponents. There was a public gallery, frequently packed with the activists of the Jacobin Club, who alternated between applauding their fellows amongst the radical *Montagnards,* and vociferously denouncing or intimidating their opponents of the Plain.

The bulk of the Moderates were intensely ambitious, and were often accused of lacking convictions or even principles, though they themselves did not see anything very principled in using the forces of armed thuggery to oust their opponents, as the Jacobins seemed to want to do. The Convention had been elected to provide France with a workable constitution, but in practice it was forced into more urgent matters: the effective prosecution of the war, the proclamation of the Republic and the trial and execution of the King, together with a whole raft of emergency legislation such as the establishment of the Committee of Public Safety and the enactment of maximum prices.

The differences between the two sides became steadily more evident, and their relations more embittered. The French armies had originally performed well at Valmy and Jemappes, but in March 1793 Dumouriez was defeated at Neerwinden, and, failing to persuade his troops to march back to Paris to proclaim Louis XVII as King, handed over to the enemy the Convention's Commissioners sent to investigate him and deserted to the Austrians. This threw into question the entire motives of those on the Moderate side. The Commune and the National Guard took the lead in demanding the overthrow of the 'Girondin faction', and on 2 June the Convention was browbeaten into decreeing the arrest of 29 deputies and two Girondin ministers. Many of the Girondins fled to the provinces, where they set about organising opposition to the Jacobin-dominated Convention; but 21 of those arrested were later executed by the Revolutionary Tribunal, along with the Duke of Orleans, Bailly, Barnave, Mme. Roland and the Queen.

## A The Jacobin View of Citizens' Rights

20 The law must be equal for all...

27 Resistance to oppression is the consequence of the other rights of man and the citizen.

28 There is oppression against the social body when a single one of its members is oppressed.

29 When the government violates the rights of the people, insurrection is the most sacred of rights and the most indispensable of duties for the people.

30 When the social guarantee is lacking to a citizen, he returns to the natural right of defending all his rights himself...

32 Public functions may not be considered as distinctions or rewards, but only as public duties.

33 Offences of the mandatories of the people must be punished severely and promptly. The people have a right to know what these mandatories are doing; they must render a faithful account of their activities and must submit to the public judgment respectfully.

34 The men of all countries are brothers, and the different peoples must help one another, according to their power, as citizens of the same state.

35 Whoever oppresses a single nation declares himself the enemy of all.

36 Whoever makes war on a people to check the progress of liberty...
must be prosecuted by all, not as ordinary enemies, but as assassins
and brigands.

from Robespierre's *Proposed Declaration of Rights,* 24 April 1793

## B   The Brissotins and the War
(i) The war with England attracts all our concern and absorbs all our
attention. Everything seems to make it certain; however, when one
considers that fundamentally there is no real motive, and when one
also sees the immense wealth gained by this nation whilst we wage
war, one is completely surprised by the folly of the cabinet of St
James.[1] Whatever may be its intention, we have to face and prepare
for it.
Note.   1 The British Government.

from a *Letter* of J.P. Brissot, 10 January 1793

(ii) Let us on this occasion rise to the full height of our mission...
      Let us say to Europe that the French would like peace, but that if
they are forced to draw the sword, they will cast away the scabbard
and will not seek it again until they are crowned with the laurels of
victory... Let us say to Europe that we will respect the constitutions of
all states, but that if the cabinets of foreign courts attempt to incite a
war of kings against France, we will incite a war of the people against
kings. (Applause.)
      Let us say to them that ten million Frenchmen, kindled by the fire
of liberty, armed with the sword, with reason, with eloquence, would
be able, if incensed, to change the face of the world and make the
tyrants tremble on their thrones.

Isnard, a leading Girondin, calls for a Crusade against Tyrants, March
1792

## C   Robespierre and the War
I, too, want war, but in a way demanded by the national interest: let
us first destroy our enemies within, and then march against the
enemy without, if any still remains... The Court and the Ministry want
war and the execution of the plan they propose to you. The nation
will accept war if it is the necessary price of liberty; but it wants, if
possible, both liberty and peace, and it rejects any plan for war whose
object might be to destroy liberty and the constitution, even if it is put
forward under the pretext of defending them. What is the war that we
are faced with? Is it a war of one nation against other nations, or of
one king against other kings? No: it is a war of the enemies of the
French Revolution against that revolution. Are the most numerous, the
most dangerous, of these enemies at Coblenz?[1] No, they are in our
own midst. Is it not reasonable to fear that we might find some of

them in the Court and in the Ministry itself?...

This is not the moment to declare war. Before all else, this is the moment to manufacture arms, in every place and at every hour; to arm the National Guard; to arm the people, if only with pikes; to adopt severe measures, and not such as have been adopted up to now, so that it will not be left to ministers to neglect with impunity what the security of the state demands: to uphold the dignity of the people and defend its too long neglected rights... It is the moment to punish the guilty ministers and persist in our determination to repress the seditious clergy.

Note 1. The centre of émigré agitation.

Robespierre, in a speech to the Jacobin Club, 18 December 1791

## D   The Girondin-Jacobin Conflict

(i) Friends, we are betrayed! To arms! To arms! This is the terrible hour when the defenders of the Motherland must conquer or be enslaved beneath the ruins of the Republic. Frenchmen, never has your liberty been in greater peril; the base treachery of our enemies has at last reached its climax, and to complete it Dumouriez, their accomplice, is marching on Paris. The manifest treasons of the generals allied with him leave no doubt that this plan of rebellion and this insolent audacity are directed by the criminal conspiracy which has maintained and deified him as it did Lafayette, and which has deceived us, up to the decisive moment, concerning the conduct, conspiracies and outrages of this traitor, who has just effected the arrest of the four Commissioners of the Convention, and now intends to dissolve it...

But, brothers and friends, these are not your only dangers; you must be convinced of an even sadder fact: your greatest enemies are in your midst; they direct your operations and reprisals; they control your means of defence!... This sacrilegious cabal is directed by the English court, and others...

It is against Paris that Dumouriez directs his vengeance, rallying to his party all the Royalists, the Feuillants, the Moderates and all the craven enemies of liberty. Therefore, it is in Paris that we must all defend it!

*Circular* from the Paris Jacobins to local branches of the Club, 5 April 1793

(ii) We recognise solemnly that the majority of the Convention is guiltless, because it has struck down the tyrant. We do not ask for the panic-stricken dissolution of the Convention or the suspension of the machinery of government; far from us is this truly anarchic idea;... we come to arouse the cry of vengeance which will be repeated throughout the whole of France...

The general assembly of the Sections of Paris, having thoroughly discussed the conduct of the deputies of the Convention, has decided that those in the list below have openly violated the trust of their constituents. Brissot, Guadet, Vergniaud, Gensonné, Grangeneuve, Buzot, Barbaroux, Salles, Biroteau, Pontécoulant, Pétron, Lanjuinais, Valzé, Hardy, Lehardy, Jean-Baptiste Louvet, Gorsas, Fauchet, Lanthenas, Lasource, Valady, Chambon.

*Address* by the Commune of Paris to the Convention, 15 April 1793

(iii) Citizens, when virtuous men... content themselves with lamenting the misfortunes of the Motherland, then perfidious persons and scoundrels become active for its destruction. If you had listened to me yesterday I would have told you that you were not masters of your internal police; I would have told you that, in conducting to this tribune a special deputy from the city of Bordeaux, he and I were insulted. I would have apprised you that new plots for the dissolution of the National Convention are being planned. I would have told you that, the day before yesterday, in an assembly of alleged members of the revolutionary committee, your dissolution was ordered in this manner: the assembly resolved to arrest all suspected men... and as a consequence of the arrests you would have been handed over to that misguided multitude which has been taught to love blood... How long, citizens, will you sleep thus?

How long will you leave the fate of liberty to chance? I urge you to take vigorous measures to frustrate the plots that surround you on all sides. The evil lies in anarchy, in this kind of insurrection of authorities against the Convention... Yes, I repeat, the evil lies in the existence of the Paris authorities, greedy for money and domination.

M.E. Guadet's speech to the Convention on the Paris Commune, 18 May 1793

(iv) Anyone who spoke of order was dishonoured as a royalist; anyone who spoke of laws was ridiculed as a statesman - an honourable name which became disreputable and a reason for proscription. It began with mutual abuse and ended with proscriptions. The Gironde was the final limit between light and darkness. When it was overthrown, we fell into chaos...

The National Convention itself was only a nominal assembly, a passive instrument of the Terror. The Terror isolated and stupified the deputies as it did the ordinary citizens. On entering the assembly, the mistrustful members watched their words and actions, fearful that they might be made a crime. In fact, everything mattered - the place where they sat, a gesture, a look, a murmur, a smile. Everyone flocked to the summit of the Mountain, which passed for the highest degree of republicanism.

from Antoine-Claire Thibadeau, *Memoirs on the Convention and the Directory*, 1824

**E   Ideas and Policies of the Girondin Party**
The Comte de Narbonne, the War Minister, favoured war hoping that it would pave the way for a strong military government. But the most effective of all in rousing the country to a state of warlike fervour was the new Left group in the Legislative Assembly, led by Jacques-Pierre Brissot, deputy for Eure-et-Loire, and composed of a score of deputies of whom several were from the south-western region of the Gironde, and supported outside the Chamber by a number of journalists and by Pétion, Robespierre's old comrade-in-arms, soon to be elected Mayor of Paris. From October 1791, Brissot preached an armed crusade of the peoples against the crowned heads of Europe, in the course of which the peoples, liberated by their own endeavours, would rally to the flag of revolution, while the King would be compelled to call on Brissot's supporters to take office. They also claimed that the war would bring other and more tangible benefits as well. It would end the external danger to France; it would force Louis to behave as a strictly constitutional king; it would divert the sans-culottes from their present preoccupation with food prices and direct their energies into constructive channels; and (though this point was not trumpeted quite so loudly abroad) victory in war would stabilise the currency and open up fresh markets for the commercial bourgeoisie.

from *Robespierre: Portrait of a Revolutionary Democrat* by George Rudé (1964)

**F   Was There a Girondin Party?**
The conception of the Girondins as a large and integrated party, apparently derived in part from Jacobin propaganda, has been fostered also by the deceptive ease with which a list of 'party supporters' can be compiled from the names of those whom the Montagnards proscribed...

The use of proscription lists to establish previous party member-ship is in fact essentially unsound. It presents a picture of a party at the very time when it had for all practical purposes ceased to exist...

Under examination, the party disintegrates... In practice, there was neither a recognised party leader nor an accepted policy. The supposed Girondin deputies consistently asserted their independence even at the most critical moments of the conflict with Robespierre...

Evidence even of collaboration between them during the time of the Convention is extremely slight, for the meetings at Madame Roland's salon lacked any precision of purpose and ended when her husband resigned his office in January 1793... Even in May 1793, when Montagnard pressure was at its greatest, the 'faction' was no more than a frail alliance of some fifteen deputies, men whose outlook was so identical with that of the majority of their colleagues that they can be distinguished only as personalities, individuals whose reputation, powers of oratory or personal courage marked them out above others as enemies of the Mountain.

When leadership had been won, they proved irresolute in everything but the endeavour to retain it, vacillating at all times and showing determination only in their efforts to crush Robespierre, the man who impugned their integrity and challenged their authority...

Although Robespierre's quarrel with Brissot began when he refused to acknowledge the expediency of an attack upon Austria, the root of his hostility towards the Brissotins lay in his recognition of their readiness to accept the Revolution as completed, to consort with men of rank and reputation, and so to sever themselves from the still unsatisfied lower ranks of the people...

Their failure to deal with the radicals of Paris must stand as the most serious failure of these men. The opening of the Convention appears in French history as a moment of great opportunity, which constructive statesmen might have employed to reconcile the people of Paris to the rule of an assembly lawfully elected by a more conservative countryside. Far from attempting this difficult task, those who led the majority first antagonised Paris by persecuting its delegates, and then fostered the latent hostility between the capital and the provinces to enlist provincial aid in their own interest. The ensuing crisis was checked by the Terror and by the Montagnards' alliance with the radicals of Paris, but this alliance was but a temporary incident, and Robespierre himself was to be overthrown in his turn in part because he too tried to restrain the radicals. The conflict between the national assembly and the sans-culottes was not resolved until Napoleon did what Brissot and the deputies from the Gironde had lacked the power or the decision to do, and dispersed the mob with his 'whiff of grapeshot.'

from *The Girondins* by M.J. Sydenham (1964)

# Questions

**1** What implied criticisms of the conduct of his political opponents in the Convention are evident from Robespierre's selection of points for his proposed *Declaration of Rights?* (Source A) **(6 marks)**

**2** How did Robespierre's attitude in Source C towards the impending European war differ from that of the Girondins in Sources B(i) and (ii)? **(6 marks)**

**3** How far are Sources D(i) and D(ii) in agreement in demanding a 'witch-hunt' to explain their failures in the military campaigns of the spring of 1793? **(6 marks)**

**4** How far does Source D(iii) help to explain why the Convention found itself besieged by the Paris mob at the end of May 1793?

**(6 marks)**

**5** How satisfactory is the explanation offered in Source D(iv) that the Convention was only 'a passive instrument of the Terror'? **(6 marks)**

**6** Compare Sources E and F, and explain how far you would agree with the view that the existence of the Girondin party was a myth created by the Jacobins. **(10 marks)**

# 9 ROBESPIERRE AND THE TERROR

The short period between the fall of the Girondins in June 1793 and the execution of Robespierre in July 1794 is known as the 'Terror', and is regarded by many as being the central episode in the French Revolution. Some of the machinery of the Terror was in place before the Girondins were expelled from the Convention: the Revolutionary Tribunal, the Committee of Public Safety and the area Watch Committees. There was a period of several months before the full Jacobin dictatorship was established, during which there was a steady drift towards the expedient of 'Terror.'

By September the Committee of Public Safety consisted of the twelve men who were to govern France unchallenged for the next ten months. They included Robespierre and his associates, military experts like Carnot, and other Jacobin radicals. During these months they met regularly, often at night when the work of the Convention and of the Jacobin Club was over. They transacted a vast amount of business, much of it minutely detailed, dealing with daily administration, both domestic and military.

As time went on, Robespierre found himself challenged both from the right and from the left. The sans-culottes and the Hébertists on the left demanded firm price-controls and a tightening up of security arrangements. Hébert in particular began a violent campaign against the Church, and succeeded, much against Robespierre's better judgment, in de-Christianising France, closing churches and abolishing traditional sabbath and saints' days by introducing a new non-Christian calendar. At the same time, Robespierre faced an equally serious threat from the Moderates, headed by G.J. Danton, a Jacobin who began to believe that extremism was going too far. His policy of 'clemency' was attractive to middle-class elements and had the secret support of many of the masses; and on account of its 'respectability' it was hated by Robespierre even more than the wild ravings of those on the left. The Hébertist group were generally known as the 'ultra-revolutionaries' and the Dantonist group as the 'citra-revolutionaries'.

In March, Robespierre secured the passing of a decree against conspiracies, arrested and briefly tried the Hébertists, and on the 24th sent them to the guillotine. He then moved swiftly against the Dantonists, whom he accused of graft and counter-revolution. By 5 April Danton and his colleagues had also been hastily tried and executed.

Though his personal position was now unchallenged, Robespierre still regarded terror as a necessity. In May, the Revolutionary Tribunal was reorganised so as to speed up its working, and on 10 June, by the Law of 22 Prairial, it was increased in size and sub-divided so as to move even more swiftly, whilst at the same time the accused were stripped of their rights.

The final outburst of Terror was to prove Robespierre's undoing. Everyone feared that his wrath would fall next upon them. Furthermore, two of the basic reasons for the Terror no longer existed: France was no longer in danger from her foreign enemies, and the counter-revolutionary rebellion in the Vendée had been quelled. Robespierre had been absent from meetings of the Convention for some time. On 26 July he returned to make a defiant speech against his enemies, though without naming any of them. The Convention turned against him, denied him the floor, denounced him bitterly and ordered his arrest. On 28 July he and about twenty of his associates went to the guillotine.

There followed the period known as the 'Thermidorian reaction'. Those who initiated it seem to have intended to continue the Terror in a different form rather than to end it, but the return to power of many of the more moderate elements soon changed its character, and prepared the way for a more conservative government under the Directory.

## A  Robespierre's Views on Political Policy

(i) The object of every political association is to safeguard the natural and imprescriptible rights of men, and to develop all their faculties... The most important rights of men are self-preservation and liberty... Liberty is the right of every man to exercise his faculties as he will. Its rule is justice; its limits are the rights of others; its source is nature; its guarantee is the law...The law can prohibit only what is harmful and require only what is useful to society... It is the duty of society to provide a living for all its members, either by procuring them work, or by assuring the means of subsistence to those who are unfit to work... Society ought to encourage the progress of public intelligence, and bring education within the reach of every citizen... The people is sovereign; the government is its work and its property; public officials are its agents... All citizens have an equal right to share in the appointment of the people's deputies, and in legislation.

Robespierre, in a speech on his Proposed Declaration of Rights, 24 April 1793. (See Document 8A)

(ii) The first maxim of our policy should be to guide the people by reason and repress the enemies of the people by terror. If the basis of popular government in time of peace is virtue, its basis in time of revolution is both virtue and terror – virtue, without which all terror is disastrous; and terror, without which all virtue is vain... Terror is merely justice – prompt, severe and inflexible. It is, therefore, an emanation of virtue; it is less a particular principle than a consequence of the general principles of democracy.

Robespierre on the need for Jacobin dictatorship, 5 February 1793

## B The Machinery of the Terror

(i) *Title I: Composition and Organisation* 1 A Special Criminal Court shall be established in Paris to take cognizance of all counter-revolutionary activities, all attacks on liberty, equality, unity, the indivisibility of the Republic, the internal and external security of the state, and all plots for the re-establishment of monarchy or of any other authority...

2 The court shall be composed of a jury, and of five judges who shall direct the enquiry and apply the law after the jury have declared upon the facts...

8 The functions of the police of general security, assigned to the municipalities and the administrative bodies shall extend to the crimes mentioned in Article 1 of the present decree...

12 The jurors shall vote and make their declaration publicly and aloud...

13 Decisions shall be executed without the right of appeal.

*Title II: Penalties* 2 The property of those condemned to the penalty of death shall be acquired by the Republic.

*Decree* establishing the Revolutionary Tribunal, 10 March 1793

(ii) The National Convention decrees:

1 A Committee of Public Safety, composed of nine members of the National Convention, shall be formed by roll call.

2 The Committee shall deliberate in secret, and shall be responsible for supervising and accelerating the work of administration entrusted to the Executive Council, the decrees of which it may even suspend when it believes them contrary to the national interest...

3 In critical circumstances it is authorised to take measures of general defence, both internal and external...

5 It shall make a weekly general report, in writing, of its activities and of the state of the Republic...

7 The aforementioned Committee is established for only one month.

*Decree* establishing the Committee of Public Safety, 6 April 1793

(iii) 1 Three representatives of the people shall be allotted regularly to each of the armies of the Republic; every month one of the three shall be renewed.

2 They shall exercise the most careful supervision over the activities of the agents of the Executive Council, over the conduct of the generals, officers and soldiers of the army; they shall render a daily

account of the inventory of the stores, equipment, provisions and munitions; they shall conduct the strictest examination of the activities and behaviour of all purveyors and contractors to the armies of the Republic.

*Decree* establishing Deputies on Mission, 9 April 1793

(iv) 1 The articles which the National Convention has deemed essential, and the maximum price of which it has believed it should establish, are: fresh meat, salt meat and bacon, butter, sweet oil, cattle, salt fish, wine, brandy, vinegar, cider, beer, firewood, charcoal, coal, candles, lamp oil, salt, soda, sugar, honey, white paper, hides, iron, cast iron, lead, steel, copper, hemp, linens, woollens, stuffs, canvases, raw materials used for fabrics, wooden shoes, shoes, colza and rape, soap, potash and tobacco.
2    Among the articles in the above list, the maximum price for firewood of the first quality, that of charcoal, and of coal, are the same as in 1790, plus one-twentieth... The maximum price of tobacco in rolls is twenty sous a pound; that of smoking tobacco is ten sous; that of salt per pound is two sous, that of soap twenty-five sous.
3    The maximum price of all the other commodities specified in Article 1 for the whole extent of the Republic shall be the price which each of them had in 1790 as stated by the current prices of each department, plus one-third.

*Law* of the Absolute Maximum, 29 September 1793

(v) 1 Immediately after the publication of the present decree, all suspected persons within the territory of the Republic and still at liberty shall be placed in custody.
2    The following are deemed suspected persons: 1st, those who by their conduct, associations, talk or writings have shown themselves the partisans of tyranny or federalism and enemies of liberty; 2nd, those who are unable to justify their means of existence and the performance of their civic duties; 3rd, those to whom certificates of patriotism have been refused; 4th, public functionaries suspended or dismissed from their positions; 5th, former nobles, husbands, wives, fathers, mothers, sons or daughters, brothers or sisters and agents of the émigrés who have not steadily shown their loyalty to the Revolution...
5    Individuals arrested as suspects shall be taken first to the jails of their place of detention...
8    The expenses of custody shall be charged to the prisoners.

*Law of Suspects,* 17 September 1793

(vi) The National Convention, on the recommendation of the Committees of Public Safety and General Security, decrees:

1    All the communes of the Republic shall draft statements of the indigent patriots within their confines, giving name, age, occupation, and the number of their children...

2    When the Committee of Public Safety has received these, it shall use them as a means of indemnifying all the unfortunates with the property of the enemies of the Revolution.

The Second *Decree of Ventôse,* 3 March 1794

(vii) 1 In the Revolutionary Tribunal there shall be: a President and four Vice-presidents; one Public Prosecutor and four substitutes, and twelve judges.

2    The jurors shall be fifty in number.

3    ... The Tribunal shall divide itself into sections, composed of twelve members, to wit: three judges and nine jurors...

4    The Revolutionary Tribunal is instituted to punish the enemies of the people.

5    The enemies of the Republic are those who seek to destroy the public liberty either by force or by cunning.

7    The penalty for all offences within the jurisdiction of the Revolutionary Tribunal is death.

Decree Extending the Powers of the Revolutionary Tribunal, *(The Law of 22 Prairial),* 10 June 1794

## C    The Execution of Robespierre

On 10 Thermidor, at four o'clock in the afternoon, the sinister procession issued from the courtyard of the Palais de Justice. No crowd of such dimensions had ever been seen in Paris. The streets were choked with people. Spectators, men and women of all ages, filled the windows on all the floors, and men had climbed on to the roofs of the houses. There was universal jubilation with an admixture of fury. The long-suppressed hatred against these criminals now exploded with redoubled force. Each one of the spectators saw in them his personal enemies. Everyone applauded madly and seemed to be sorry he could not do more. Most of the watchers fixed their eyes on the cart in which the two Robespierres, Couthon and Hanriot were riding. These miserable creatures were all mutilated and covered with blood, and looked like a group of brigands whom the gendarmes had surprised in a wood and had been unable to arrest without wounding them.

It would be difficult to describe the appearance of Robespierre. His face was wrapped in a bandage of dirty, blood-stained linen, and, from what one could see of his features, was horribly disfigured. A livid pallor made it even more repulsive. He kept his eyes cast down and almost closed, but whether this was due to the pain caused by his wounds or to the consciousness of his misdeeds one cannot say.

Just before arriving at the place of execution, he was shaken out of his lethargy by a woman who forced her way through the crowd, and rushed up to the cart carrying this cannibal. She grasped the rail of the cart, and with the other hand threatened him, saying: 'Monster, spewed up from hell! The thought of your punishment intoxicates me with joy!' Robespierre opened his eyes and looked at her sadly as she added: 'Go, evildoer, go down into your grave loaded with the curses of the wives and mothers of France.'

When the cart had reached the foot of the scaffold, the executioner's assistants carried the tyrant down and laid him out prone until it was his turn for execution. It was observed that whilst his accomplices were being beheaded, he appeared not to take notice. He kept his eyes shut and did not reopen them until he felt himself being carried up on to the scaffold. Some said that when he saw the instrument of death he heaved a sigh of pain. After having thrown down his coat which was draped round his shoulders, the executioner roughly tore away the bandage and the splint which the surgeon had put on his wounds. This unshipped the lower jaw from his upper one, and caused the blood to flow profusely. The wretched man's head was now no more than an object of horror and repulsion. When at last it was severed from his body and the executioner took it by the hair to show it to the people, it presented an indescribably horrible spectacle.

Eye-witness account of Robespierre's execution, 10 Thermidor (28 July) 1794

## D The Terror : A Response to Crisis

France [in 1793] suffered from anarchy, and what it needed was government. 'Anarchy' is not too strong a word. Ministers remained in existence, but decisions lay with Committees of the Convention, which consisted of 750 men from the middle classes assembled under chaotic conditions, and enjoying neither the confidence in each other, nor the prestige of an acknowledged authority, nor habits of obedience on the part of the population. Organs of local government, set up in 1791, had not had time to consolidate. Tax reforms had been caught unfinished by the war and the upheaval of 1792. Taxes, like much else, existed mainly in principle. There were no regular revenues, so that the Convention depended on paper money. Army reforms, begun early in the Revolution, were far from complete; the country went to war with its armies commanded largely by officers of the Old Régime. Dumouriez was the most spectacular case.

Impotence in government was matched by an intense political liveliness among the 'governed'. It was a question of whether the country could be governed at all, except by dictatorship... The French people in 1793 were too highly politicised, too spontaneously active, too disillusioned with persons in public office to accept orders from any political heights. When they said the people were sovereign they meant it literally, and they meant themselves. Middle-class citizens in the Paris Jacobin Club and in similar clubs in the provinces, acting on their own initiative, tried somehow to keep going and to dominate the shattered apparatus of state, from the National Convention down to the village communes...

An extreme crisis of confidence in the political realm coincided with an extreme economic crisis. In the inflamed psychology of the moment, both crises were blamed on the same people. Suspicion was rampant. The guilty must be investigated and pursued. In March the Convention created a new special court for this purpose, the Revolutionary Tribunal, in which the civil liberties and the legal reforms introduced by the Revolution could be suspended...

Meanwhile the Convention, at war with all Europe, with its commanding general in Belgium proved disloyal, with peasants in armed rebellion in the West, with the currency out of control, the economy collapsing and the popular insurrection in the Paris Sections boiling over, found moments to engage in its theoretically principal business, to 'constitute' a regular government through a new written constitution and declaration of rights. The constitutional committee was dominated by Condorcet and other Brissotins and Girondists... Robespierre was convinced that the Girondists were unfit to govern. He made an issue over their proposed Declaration of Rights. On 24 April he submitted to the Convention a draft Declaration of his own. Though never adopted, it is a key document to the understanding of his thinking and tactics.

A constitution was thrown together in a few days. Full of elaborately democratic provisions it came to be known as the Constitution of Year I - that is, the first year of the Republic... The Convention, given the facts of war and revolution, made no move to put the Constitution into effect, seeming rather to envisage its own indefinite continuance...

Robespierre was now turning from insurrectionism to 'revolutionary governmment', and himself had a hand in this incipient government. In July the Convention elected him to the Committee of Public Safety. But matters had never been worse for the Convention than in this summer of 1793. Marat was assassinated in his bath. The great provincial cities, Lyons, Marseilles, Bordeaux, where the expulsion of the Girondists angered the urban bourgeoisie, denounced the anarchy in Paris and defied the authority of the Convention...

On the other hand, the government began to govern. The Committee of Public Safety received larger powers. Its membership settled at twelve, who remained the same individuals from September 1793 to July 1794. They included Robespierre, Saint-Just, Couthon,

Barère and Lazare Carnot...

By the spring of 1794 the French armies resumed the offensive. In June they won the battle of Fleurus, and the Austrians abandoned Belgium. In the Dutch cities, the revolutionaries took hope again... The outcome was uncertain, but in France it was clear, by mid-1794, that the Republic had survived.

from *The Age of Democratic Revolution* (Vol. II) by R.R. Palmer (1964)

# Q *uestions*

1 How does Robespierre in Sources A(i)-(ii) reconcile liberty and coercion? **(5 marks)**

2 Using the source and your own knowledge, explain why the Law of the Absolute Maximum (Source B(v)) was so ineffective. **(6 marks)**

3 'The Terror was more than the shedding of blood; it was a system of government.' What evidence in Sources B(i)-(vii) gives support to this view? **(9 marks)**

4 What evidence is there that Source C was written by a political opponent? How far would such opposition undermine the historical reliability of the source? **(5 marks)**

5 What, according to Source D, were the main reasons for the Terror? **(5 marks)**

6 Use Sources C and D, and your own knowledge, to show how assessments of Robespierre's role during the Terror have been modified with the passage of time. **(10 marks)**

# 10 WAR AND THE RISE
## OF THE NATIONAL STATE

From 1792 to 1815, an entire generation of Frenchmen was continuously at war. From the earliest disorganised beginnings, when a plaintive note of grievance and a whiff of revolutionary propaganda crept into France's denunciations of its more powerful neighbours, through to the harsh imperious tones in which Napoleon addressed Europe, the French government gradually grew in strength and self-confidence. During these years its effectiveness developed, and the areas which it sought to regulate and command, marked it apart from earlier styles of government: under it the words 'sovereign' and 'totalitarian' take on a new meaning. By comparison, the *Ancien Régime,* earlier denounced as a thorough-paced despotism, was distinguished by its casualness, its incompleteness and its tentativeness. Yet, as it grew, the revolutionary government tended to ride roughshod over the individual rights of the very people it had originally sought to champion.

This poses a central problem: was the French Revolution driven from the paths of democracy by its total immersion in foreign war after 1792; or was the Revolution so steeped in Rousseau's ideas of the General Will, or the idea of the 'indivisibility' of freedom and the 'paramountcy' of the Nation, that any attempt to introduce a participatory democracy was bound to fail, quite irrespective of war?

There is some truth in both views. On the one hand, foreign war drove political leaders to take a tough line with their own supporters if the Revolution was to survive: the Girondins, many of whom still favoured a monarchy, had to threaten to discipline the Paris sections and perished in the attempt; the Jacobins introduced a 'police state' and yet fell because of the hostility of the masses; and the Thermidorians and the Directory, fearful of the anarchy and violence which mob-rule could bring, moved back from the brink and once more began to buttress legal authority. Yet they were only able to do this because they had significant military support , from the 'Whiff of Grapeshot' in the coup of Vendémiaire 1795 to the successful coup of Brumaire in 1799.

On the other hand, there was a powerful centralising tendency at work that seemed in line with the teachings of rationalist philosophy. The desire for simplicity, uniformity, and rationality could be seen at work throughout the period in almost the whole of the legislation enacted. This philosophic impulse towards centralisation, forced the French to persist in their efforts on behalf of the new order even when it eroded popular hopes of greater freedom. Fraternity and equality, neither of them specially libertarian, together with military pre-eminence, came to be the focus of French hopes.

## A   Foreign Feelings about the Revolution

(i) I am sure Your Majesty will have learned of the unprecedented outrage of the arrest of the King of France, of my sister the Queen, and of the Royal Family, with as much surprise and indignation as I have, and that your sentiments cannot differ from mine with regard to an event which, inspiring fear of still more dreadful ones to follow, and placing the mark of illegality upon previous excesses in France, immediately compromises the honour of all sovereigns and the security of all governments.

Determined to fulfil my obligation in these respects, both as chosen Head of the Germanic Body and as Sovereign of the Austrian States, I propose to the Kings of Spain, England, Prussia, Naples and Sardinia, as well as to the Empress of Russia, a union amongst themselves and with me for counsel, co-operation, and measures to restore the liberty and honour of the Most Christian King and his Family, and to limit the dangerous extremes of the French Revolution.

*Signed* Leopold

from the Padua Circular, 5 July 1791

(ii) His Majesty the Emperor and His Majesty the King of Prussia, having heard the requests of... M. le Comte d'Artois, jointly declare that they regard the present position of His Majesty the King of France as a matter of common concern to all the sovereigns of Europe. They trust that the powers whose aid is supplicated will not fail to recognise this fact; and that accordingly they will not refuse to co-operate with their said Majesties in employing, in proportion to their forces, the most effective means for enabling the King of France to consolidate with complete freedom the foundations of a monarchical government, equally suited to the rights of sovereigns and the welfare of the French nation.

Leopold          Frederick William

from The Declaration of Pillnitz, 27 August 1791

(iii) Since their Majesties, the Emperor and the King of Prussia, have entrusted me with the command of their combined armies on the frontiers of France, I have resolved to announce to the inhabitants of that kingdom the motives that have decided the actions of the two sovereigns and the intentions guiding them...

Convinced that the main part of the French nation abhors the excesses of the faction dominating it, and that the majority of them impatiently await the moment of relief in order to declare openly against the odious conduct of its oppressors, their Majesties summon and invite them to return without delay to ways of reason, justice, order and peace. It is in accordance with these views that I, general commander of the two armies, declare:

1st That the two allied courts propose no other aim than the welfare of France, and do not intend to enrich themselves by any conquest;

2nd That they do not intend to interfere in the internal government of France...

3rd That the combined armies will protect the cities, towns and villages, and the property and persons of all who submit...

7th That inhabitants... who dare defend themselves against our troops, and fire on them... shall be punished immediately, according to the rigour of the law of war, and their houses demolished or burned... They further declare that if the Palace of the Tuileries is entered by force or attacked, if the least outrage is done to Their Majesties, if Their security and liberty be not provided for immediately, they will exact an exemplary vengeance thereon by delivering the city of Paris to military punishment and total destruction...

For these reasons, I require all inhabitants of the kingdom... not to oppose the progress and operations of the troops which I command, but rather to grant them everywhere free entry and good will, aid and assistance.

Given at my headquarters at Coblenz, 25 July 1792

*Signed* Charles William Ferdinand, Duke of Brunswick-Lunebourg.

from the Brunswick Manifesto, 25 July 1792

**B French Reactions**
(i) The National Assembly, considering that the Court of Vienna, in contempt of treaties, has continued to grant protection to French rebels, that it has formed a concert with several European powers against the security of the French nation;

That Francis II, King of Hungary and Bohemia, has refused to renounce such concert;

That he has formally attacked the sovereignty of the French nation by declaring his wish to support the pretensions of German princes owning lands in France...

[3 other 'considerations']

The National Assembly declares that the French nation, faithful to the principles enshrined in its constitution *not to undertake any war with a view to making conquests, and never to employ its forces against the liberty of any people,* takes arms only to maintain its liberty and independence;...

Deliberating upon the formal proposal of the King... the National

Assembly declares war on the King of Hungary and Bohemia.

French Declaration of War against Austria, 20 April 1792

(ii) The National Convention, having heard the report of its Committee of General Defence concerning the conduct of the English Government towards France;
    Considering that the King of England has not ceased to give the French nation proofs of his malevolence and of his attachment to the coalition of crowned heads...
    [19 other 'considerations', including]
    That he has drawn into the same coalition the Stadtholder of the United Provinces, whose servile devotion to the orders of the Cabinet of St James and of Berlin is only too notorious...
    Considering, lastly, that all these circumstances leave the French Republic no longer any hope of obtaining the redress of its grievances by means of amicable negotiations;...
    The National Convention declares, in the name of the French Nation, that... the French Republic is at war with the King of England and the Stadtholder of the United Provinces.

French Declaration of War against England and Holland, 1 February 1793

## C French Government Defence Policies
(i) The National Assembly, having declared urgency, decrees as follows:
    1st The armed force shall be increased by 20 000 men.
    2nd Such increase shall be effected in the departments, and all cantons of the kingdom shall be allowed to contribute thereto.
    3rd The additional 20 000 men shall assemble in Paris for 14 July next.

Decree for the Formation of an Army of 20 000 *Fédérés,* 8 June 1792

(ii) *Title I* 1 The National Assembly summons 300 000 men who shall join the armies of the Republic as soon as possible...
    9 As soon as the officials who have received the statement of the men whom their commune is to furnish, they shall give notice thereof to the citizens who are to be convoked for such purpose...
    11 In the event that voluntary enrolment does not yield the number of men requested from each commune, the citizens shall be required to complete it at once; and for such purpose they shall adopt the method they find most suitable.
    12 The complement shall be taken only from among bachelors and widowers without children between the ages of eighteen and forty years inclusive.

Decree for a Levy of 300 000 men, 24 February 1793

(iii) 1 Henceforth, until the enemies have been driven from the territories of the Republic, the French people are in permanent requisition for army service.

The young men shall go to battle; the married men shall forge arms and transport provisions; the women shall make tents and clothes; the children shall turn old linen into lint; the old men shall stimulate the courage of the warriors and preach the unity of the Republic and hatred of kings.

2 National buildings shall be converted into barracks; public places into armament workshops; the soil of cellars shall be washed in strong alkaline solution to extract saltpetre therefrom...

7 No one may pay for a substitute in the service to which he is called...

8 The levy shall be general. Unmarried citizens or childless widowers from eighteen to twenty-five years shall go first; they shall meet without delay in the chief town of their districts, where they shall exercise daily while awaiting the time for departure.

Decree for a *Levée en Masse*, 23 August 1793

(iv) The Council... considering that it is essential to give the military forces of the French Republic as full development as its population warrants, so that it may always triumph over its enemies... approves the act of urgency and this resolution.

*Title I* 1 Every Frenchman is a soldier, and owes it to himself to defend the Motherland...

3 The army shall be constituted by voluntary enlistment and by military conscription...

*Title III* 15 Military conscription includes all Frenchmen between the ages of twenty and twenty-five years...

19 The conscripts... may not have substitutes.

First General Conscription Law, 5 September 1798

**D French War Aims**
(i) The National Convention declares, in the name of the French Nation, that it will grant fraternity and aid to all peoples who wish to recover their liberty; and it charges the executive power with giving the generals the orders necessary for bringing aid to such peoples, and for defending citizens who have been, or might be, harassed for the cause of liberty.

First Decree of Fraternity, 19 November 1792

(ii) 1 In territories which are or may be occupied by the armies of the Republic, the generals shall proclaim immediately, in the name of the French nation, the sovereignty of the people...

2 They shall announce to the people that they bring it peace, aid, fraternity, liberty and equality...

7 The Executive Council shall appoint national commissioners... to consult the generals and the provisional administration elected by the people concerning measures to be taken for common defence and concerning the means to be used to procure the clothing and provisions necessary for the armies...

10 A statement shall be made of the expenses which the French Republic has incurred for the common defence and of the sums which it may have received, and the French nation shall make arrangements with the established government for whatever is due.

Second Decree of Fraternity, 15 December 1792

## E Patriotism on the March
Come, children of the Motherland, the day of glory has arrived!
Against us, the tyrant has raised his sanguinary banner,
Has raised his sanguinary banner!
Don't you hear across our countryside the roar of his merciless soldiery?
They are coming right into your arms to butcher your friends and family!
Citizens, to arms! Form up your battalions!
Let's march! March! So that our very fields shall wash with their evil blood!
Wash with their evil blood!

The Marching Song of the Men from Marseilles, 1792

## F The Development of the Centralised Modern State
It should be noted that the problems posed by the rise of both the right and the left contributed in no small measure to the significant growth of a strong centralised French state during the 1790s. From all the eddies of revolution and war, one current flowing throughout the 1790s may be discerned - the increasing determination of the wealthy, commercial, industrial but predominantly landed élites to 'save' the Revolution, Rousseauesque or not, from the radical popular masses in Paris as well as from the 'reactionary' popular masses in the Vendée and the south-east... It was in the pursuit of their objective of reshaping France in their own image that the propertied classes would realise that a strong state was essential. However, widespread political apathy and administrative instability during the late 1790s undermined moves in this direction, creating the political circumstances for a series of coups d'état. By 1799, the army was the only agency which could save both the bourgeois revolution of the property-owners, as well as France itself...

The fact that the Constitution of 1793 was stillborn underlines the immense gap... which separated the political idealism of 1789 from the harsh socio-economic and military facts of life in that summer of 1793, when Jacobins and sans-culottes began to dominate the political scene in most towns and villages of France, a sword in one hand and social policy in the other. The great political paradox of Year II was that whilst the Jacobins, desperate to unleash the energies of the nation for war, sought to satisfy the social and economic aspirations of the urban and rural masses, they were also creating the structures of a powerful state bureaucracy, civil and military, which would eventually be used to eject the mass of the public from a participatory democracy.

from *The French Revolution: Rethinking the Debate* by Gwynne Lewis (1993)

### G  The Impact of the French Revolutionary Wars

The French revolutionary wars constituted the first modern war, not because it represented a conflict between two diametrically opposed ideologies, but because of what it became. By liberating their state in the course of 1792-94, by casting off all inhibitions and maximising their resources, the French revolutionaries waged total war of unprecedented intensity and on an unprecedented scale. Not only did it 'revolutionize the revolution', it also forced the other European states into emulation, however delayed and partial. After almost a quarter of a century of devastation, exploitation and over-exertion, no part of Europe was untouched: politically, economically, socially, intellectually or culturally. It was not the French Revolution which created the modern world, it was the French revolutionary wars.

from *The Origins of the French Revolutionary Wars* by T.C.W. Blanning (1986)

## Q *uestions*

1  (a)  How serious was the threat which the Emperor Leopold II posed to the French nation in Sources A(i) and A(ii)?  **(4 marks)**

   (b)  The Brunswick Manifesto (Source A(iii)) cause panic in Paris. Was this panic justified by the Manifesto's contents?  **(4 marks)**

2  'A war of ideologies.' Is this judgment on the Revolutionary War borne out by Sources B(i) and B(ii)?  **(6 marks)**

3  (a)  Are Sources C(i) to C(iii) adequate to explain the French military success of 1794?  **(4 marks)**

   (b)  Explain how differently Frenchmen were affected by the military laws of 1792-3 and the law of September 1798.  **(4 marks)**

**4** (a) Comparing Sources D(i) and D(ii), explain in what ways the French government so swiftly changed its mind about its attitudes towards occupied lands at the end of 1792. **(4 marks)**

(b) Use your own knowledge to explain why the British government was so alarmed at the contents of both Decrees of Fraternity.

**(4 marks)**

**5** In its own way, Source E was 'an appeal to ideology.' How far do you agree? **(4 marks)**

**6** How far does Blanning's argument in Source G justify the judgment he makes in his final sentence? **(8 marks)**

**7** To what extent do the sources in this unit support the view in Source F that the fate of the Revolution from 1793 was to be in the hands of the military, rather than the politicians? **(8 marks)**

# 11 THE DIRECTORY

The fall of Robespierre took place at the end of July 1794. It was followed by the reversal of many of the policies of the Terror, and included efforts directed against the Jacobin Club and the 'insurrectionary' Paris Commune. The royalists, who were glad to see the Jacobins overthrown, now hoped to profit from a complete reaction in politics. The 'Thermidorians', however, were in most cases revolutionaries themselves, and supporters of many Jacobin measures. But the Constitution of 1793 was a good deal too democratic for even the Jacobins, and was hardly likely to be enforced by the Thermidorians.

Instead, they brought in a new Constitution of the Year III, under which the Directory was set up in 1795. It tried to provide France with stable government without destroying the Revolution. In place of the single assembly, the Constitution established a Legislature of two houses: the Council of the Five Hundred, and the Council of Elders; executive powers was entrusted to five Directors, one of whom was to be replaced each year. In their anxiety to avoid a swing back to the right, and in order to ensure the continuance of their own power, the outgoing government required that two thirds of the new assemblies should be chosen from the old Convention; these were promptly dubbed the 'Perpetuals' by their critics.

This Constitution soon ran into trouble. In their anxiety to prevent it from being tampered with, its drafters had made the Constitution very difficult to amend. This rigidity itself soon presented a problem.

The Directory began with a royalist rising in Vendémiaire (October 1795), which the young Napoleon dispersed with his 'Whiff of Grapeshot'. Another followed on 18 Fructidor (4 September) 1797, when the 'Old Guard' in the Councils and the Directory purged royalist councillors and annulled the election of some 200 of those recently voted in. Something similar happened on 22 Floréal (11 May) 1798, except that this time it was radical Jacobins who were purged. In the last of these coups, that of 30 Prairial (18 June) 1798, it was the newly-elected 'Republicans' who took the initiative and purged the Directory. This was followed by a number of rigorous items of legislation which the Directors could not check. The sorry story of the Directory came to an end with the Coup d'état of Brumaire (9-10 November) 1799, when one of the new Directors, Sieyès, looking for a military man to help him liquidate the opposition and create a stronger executive, found one in Bonaparte, recently returned from his Egyptian Campaign. Together they replaced the Directory with the Consulate, which was to last until the creation of the Empire in 1804.

Nevertheless, the Directory accomplished a great deal. In finance, the Directory did much to rescue the country from bankruptcy and hyperinflation. The assignats, now almost worthless, were cancelled and metallic currency reintroduced. At the same time, the public debt was reduced by two-thirds in September 1797. Soon after, the tax system was completely overhauled. The new system was based on four direct taxes which eventually filled the state's coffers and did away with the corruption which had become a feature of the unreformed system. In administration, the basis of the modern civil service was laid. Weights and measures were standardised and rationalised. Education was reformed, as were the army and the hospitals. The Directory did not resolve religious difficulties, but cleared the way for their solution under the Consulate. All these reforms were impaired by the pressures of war, lack of adequate funds and recurrent political instability, but they helped to provide a framework for the modern French political system.

## A  Vilifying Robespierre

For several months a single man, strengthened by usurped popularity and enormous influence, ruled like a despot over the government or blocked its course; tyrannised the Convention or debased it; raised himself above the law or shamelessly dictated it; made himself master of public opinion or destroyed it to replace it with his own; oppressed patriots and prescribed everything that had integrity and virtue; set up tribunals and dictated their verdicts to them; protected scoundrels and intriguers; filled the offices of constituted authorities with his creatures; in this way seized civil and military power to make them serve his whims and furies. In brief, Robespierre aroused dark suspicion, cruel distrust, alarms, terror in all hearts; he separated man from man and carried out the maxim of all tyrants: divide and rule!

Speech of one of Robespierre's opponents in the Convention, July 1794

## B  The Thermidorian Reaction

1   The Revolutionary Tribunal shall have cognizance of all attacks upon the internal and external security of the state, the liberty, equality, unity and indivisibility of the Republic, and the national representation...

3   The criminal courts shall continue to have cognizance, concurrently with the Revolutionary Tribunal, of counter-revolutionary offences...

21  No one may be arraigned before the Revolutionary Tribunal except:

By a decree of the National Convention;

Or by order of the Committee of General Security;

Or by warrant of arrest issued by the Tribunal or by the Public

Prosecutor...

28 In every action brought before the Revolutionary Tribunal, at least twenty-four hours before pleadings are begun, one of the magistrates... shall have the defendant brought before him, shall inform him of the indictment, shall have a copy delivered to him, shall question him on the facts stated therein, shall receive his replies, and shall advise him that the law permits him to choose a counsel...

67 If the accused is found not guilty, the President shall announce that he is acquitted of the charge, and shall order that he be set free immediately...

69 Any person thus acquitted may never again be arrested or indicted on the same charge.

*Decree* Reorganising the Revolutionary Tribunal, 28 December 1794

## C  Attempted Coups under the Directory

(i) At last it is all over; my first impulse is to let you hear from me.

The royalists, constituted in Sections, were daily becoming bolder. The Convention gave orders that the Lepelletier Section should be disarmed; it repulsed the troops. It was said that Menou, the commander, was a traitor; he was dismissed immediately. The Convention appointed Barras to command the armed forces; the Committees chose me as second-in-command. We disposed our troops; the enemy attacked us at the Tuileries; we killed a large number of them; they killed thirty of our men and wounded sixty. We have disarmed the Sections, and all is quiet. As usual, I was unharmed.

*Letter* of Napoleon to his brother Joseph Bonaparte, 6 October 1795, the day after the crushing of the Rising of Vendémiaire (by the 'Whiff of Grapeshot')

(ii) The French people have entrusted the custody of their Constitution primarily to the fidelity of the Legislative Body and the executive power.

The integrity of such confidence has been threatened by a royalist plot, organised long since, woven with skill and pursued with tenacity. The Directory has discovered this plot; the guilty parties have been apprehended; the Legislative Body has promptly taken the measures which circumstances demanded.

Blood has not been shed; wisdom has governed force; valour and discipline have moderated the use thereof. National justice has been consecrated by the composure of the people...

The Legislative Body and the Directory have performed their duty...

Be impressed by this great example...

Thanks to your destiny, the conspirators no longer exist, either in the Directory or in the two Councils. The Councils and the Directory proceed harmoniously, and the Republic is saved. Long live the Republic!

*Proclamation* of the Directory to the French People after the Coup d'état of Fructidor, 9 September 1797

**D  The Aftermath of the Coup d'état of Prairial**
(i) Any authority or any individual who makes an attack on the security or the liberty of the Legislative Body, or upon any of its members, either by giving or carrying out an order, shall be outlawed.

Law of 30 Prairial, 18 June 1799

(ii) 2   The kinsmen of *émigrés,* their relatives by marriage and former nobles, the grandfathers, grandmothers, fathers and mothers of persons who, without being nobles, of kinsmen or *émigrés* are nevertheless notoriously known as taking part in gatherings or bands of assassins, are personally responsible for assassinations and acts of brigandage, out of hatred of the Republic, in the departments declared in a state of disturbance.
3   The central administrations shall take hostages from the classes above designated...
4   The hostages shall be established at their own expense...
11   The property of deported hostages shall be placed under sequestration.

Law of Hostages, 18 June 1799

**E   The Coup d'état of Brumaire**
(i) The Council, considering the situation of the Republic, approves the act of urgency and the following resolution:
1   The Directory no longer exists; and the individuals hereinafter named are no longer members of the national representation because of the excesses and crimes in which they have continually engaged... [There follows a list of sixty-one names.].
2   The Legislative Body creates provisionally an Executive Consular Commission, composed of citizens Sieyès and Roger Ducos, former Directors, and Bonaparte, General, who shall bear the names of Consuls of the French Republic.

Brumaire Decree, 10 November 1799

(ii) Napoleon on 19 Brumaire, by François Bouchot The 19th Brumaire.
His speech has been shouted down by angry members of the Five
Hundred, and grenadiers prepare to escort Napoleon from the Hall.

(iii) On my return to Paris I found division among all authorities, and agreement upon one point, namely, that the Constitution was half destroyed and unable to save liberty.

All parties came to me, confided to me their designs, disclosed their secrets, and requested my support; I refused to be a man of party...

I presented myself at the Council of Five Hundred, alone, unarmed, my head uncovered, just as the Elders had received and applauded me; I came to remind the majority of its wishes, and to assure it of its power...

The factions, intimidated, dispersed and fled. The majority, freed from their attacks, returned freely and peaceably into the meeting hall, deliberated, and passed the salutary resolution which is to become the provisional law of the Republic.

Frenchmen, you will doubtless recognise in this conduct the zeal of a soldier of liberty, a citizen devoted to the Republic. Conservative, protective, and liberal ideas have been restored to their rights through the dispersal of the rebels who oppressed the Councils.

Bonaparte's statement on becoming Consul, 10 November 1799

(iv) Frenchmen! A Constitution is presented to you.

It terminates the uncertainties which the provisional government introduced into external relations, into the internal and military situation of the Republic...

The Constitution is founded on the true principles of representative government, on the sacred rights of property, equality and liberty.

The powers which it institutes will be strong and stable, as they must be in order to guarantee the rights of citizens and the interests of the state.

Citizens, the Revolution is established upon the principles which began it: it is ended.

Proclamation of the Consuls to the French People, 15 December 1799

## F  The Role of the Directory

(i) It is not difficult to see why, in the past, the Directors have been so harshly treated. The assumption that the Directors were themselves not exempt from the vices of corruption and immorality characteristic of French society at that date came to be identified in the popular mind with Barras. This impression of Barras as representative of the general standards of the Directory, although entirely erroneous, was to some extent intelligible. Of the thirteen individuals who at various times held office as Directors, Barras alone succeeded in retaining his position throughout, and was undoubtedly the most colourful personality of them all. The danger of generalising from the single case of Barras is, however, obvious. Another reason why injustice has been done to the Directory is that French history between 1795 and 1799 has tended to be studied by historians, very largely for the sake of convenience, as a period of *coups d'état.* This approach has had two unfortunate results. On the one hand, it has gained general acceptance for the impression that the age was one of perpetual crisis, thus distracting attention from the more solid achievements of the Directory; and, on the other, it has led to the supposition that it was this series of illegal expedients alone which secured its survival... Lastly, the reputation of the Directors may have suffered because it has been blackened by the apologists of Robespierre and the admirers of Bonaparte. Between Mathiez, who spent a lifetime defending the Jacobin leader, and Madelin, equally intent on eulogising Bonaparte, the Directors have come in for a good deal of unmerited abuse...

Whether or not Frenchmen were willing on the eve of Brumaire to exchange the republican constitution of the Year III for a military dictatorship cannot be decided with certainty. The difficulties encountered with the Council of the Five Hundred at St Cloud on 19 Brumaire, the cries of 'Outlaw him!' which greeted Bonaparte and the well-known sympathies of the Parisian troops, at least make it clear that the Constitution was still regarded as a bulwark against dictatorship. Bonaparte's military prestige had been somewhat tarnished by his abandonment of the army in Egypt, and little was known of his administrative ability. As a peace-maker, he still enjoyed the reputation he had gained at Leoben and Campo Formio, but Sieyès evidently thought that he would be willing to accept subordinate political office... The theory of an 'inevitable' military dictatorship has had a long innings; has not the time arrived when it should be abandoned? France in the autumn of 1799 was prosperous, the danger of invasion had already been averted, the reforms of Ramel and Neufchâteau were beginning to bear fruit, and the fear of reviving Jacobinism, dating back to the Law of Hostages, might easily have been dealt with in the usual way. In religious matters it is difficult to believe the persecution of the priests was any more effective in practice than the measures taken to ensure public order, and although the desire for a restoration of the altars may have been pressing, there was considerable anxiety lest with it there should be associated a return of church lands.

If Bonaparte had been forty instead of thirty, would he not have remained faithful to his original idea of becoming a Director?

from *The French Executive Directory - A Revaluation* by Albert Goodwin (1937)

(ii) If the liberal experiment of the Constitution of Year III had turned out badly, the barrier it had set up against democracy had proved to be solid: power remained in the hands of the liberal bourgeoisie...

Under Bonaparte's eyes, the bourgeoisie continued its work: it was the bourgeoisie that established the institutions of the Consulate and the Empire, and drew up the laws, thus fixing the framework of the society it dominated. The 18 Brumaire consecrated the Revolution in the form which the bourgeoisie had conceived it in 1789.

Yet the fact remains that it contained terrible disappointments for that class. One was easy to foresee. In setting up a dictatorship aimed against its enemies, the bourgeoisie had not intended to abandon freedom for itself or to subject itself to despotic control; but since the *coup d'état* was carried out by the army, who could prevent its leader from perpetrating more? The Brumairians imagined that the conservative Senate would suffice to thwart him; on the contrary, it was the chief instrument of usurpation...

But of all that imagination dreamed or produced - a new dynasty, the partial restoration of the *ancien régime,* the European Empire - nothing has remained: Napoleon has disappeared like a meteor. What has endured is the predominance of the notables, the work they completed under his guidance, the final consolidation of the Revolution which, by making a dictatorship useless in future, made it possible to begin the liberal experiment again in 1814. This is the real significance of the 18 Brumaire: initiated by a few bold bourgeois, it finally established the power of the bourgeoisie.

from *The Directory* by Georges Lefebvre and Albert Mathiez (1965)

(iii) The Directory was not a betrayal of the Revolution, but an attempt to continue its liberal ideals. It was still a revolutionary régime... keen to carry the Revolution to the rest of Europe. The 'policy of balance' itself was inherited from Year II, foreshadowed by Robespierre's Janus-like prescription of the Indulgents and the Hébertistes.

The strong Centre party, however, whose moderate Republicanism would provide a guarantee of support for a liberal régime, did not emerge. The Directory failed to establish a legitimate form of parliamentary government which could maintain the social gains of the Revolution against Royalist counter-revolution, and defend property rights against Jacobin-inspired social democracy. The development of a liberal political system, based on free elections and open discussion, required a period of calm and stability, and a consensus of agreement in favour of a moderate Republican form of government. These conditions were lacking...

Because of its difficulties, the Directory had to improvise, and on many occasions to resign itself to the government's impotence in the provinces. It was above all in its fiscal and administrative reforms that the Directory's successes were most enduring. The régime gave France a remodelled civil service and a new tax structure. In addition, it left posterity the École Polytechnique, the metre, the kilogram and the franc, smallpox vaccine and Charenton.[1] In its experimental search for Republican forms of art, education, science and religion, in its combative spirit of anti-clericalism, the Directory represented the final flowering of eighteenth-century humanism.

Note 1. An asylum for the mentally disturbed.

from France Under the Directory by Martyn Lyons (1975)

# Questions

**1** What importance should be attached to Source A by the historian?

(4 marks)

**2** Source B is strong evidence of the end of the Terror. Do you agree?

(6 marks)

**3** How far are Sources E(i) and F(i) at variance with Napoleon's own account of what happened at Brumaire in Source E(iii)? (6 marks)

**4** What evidence can you find in Sources A-E to explain why the Directory was so comparatively short-lived? (9 marks)

**5** Either: (a) Show how far the evaluations of the Directory offered in Sources F(i)-(iii) are consistent with one another.

Or: (b) Select one of Sources F(i)-(iii), and show how far its evaluation of the Directory is consistent with the view put forward in the last sentence of Source E(iv). (10 marks)

# 12 THE SOCIAL ACHIEVEMENTS
## OF THE FRENCH REVOLUTION

The Revolution was born, lived and died in a state of bankruptcy. In August 1788 the Royal government suspended the payment of interest on its debts, thus in effect acknowledging its insolvency; in September 1797, the Directory wiped out two-thirds of what it owed in the 'Law of the Consolidated Third.' The whole history of revolutionary finance was one of catastrophe. Economic policy wavered uncertainly between traditional protectionism and the currently more fashionable free trade, driven one way and then the other by inflation, chronic bread shortages and, of course, war. There were mercantilist elements in the decrees relating to the provisioning of Paris and the other major cities, as there were in enactments relating to the management of French shipping; but these were at least as much due to pressure of circumstances as to philosophy. Other measures, such as the two laws of the Maximum, foreshadowed twentieth-century efforts to construct a controlled economy and proved equally disastrous.

Yet the overall situation was not beyond repair: efforts to remedy it were constructive, and tinged with optimism. The legislation of the summer of 1789, struggling to wipe out feudalism and to construct a more rational alternative social system, perhaps mercifully failed to appreciate the gravity of the problems it was creating; nevertheless it produced measures, like the divorce law, which were astonishingly liberal for their day. It went on to equally radical measures relating to public relief; making also great strides both in the theory and the practice of education.

Of course, there were a number of proposals, for example relative to the abolition of the Christian faith and the rationalisation of the calendar and the clock, which were so grossly unrealistic (or 'philosophical' in Burke's sense of the word) that their failure could early be predicted. Such follies help to explain the fear, dismay or the contempt with which many foreign observers regarded the Revolution.

Yet it cannot be denied that in some aspects of life the Revolution generated great energy. But in music, pictorial art, costume, sculpture or architecture, none of this was specially creative; the classical theme ran strongly through it all, echoing the ancient Roman Republic. But one of the most surprising things about the Revolution is that, in spite of the monstrous difficulties with which it was faced, it threw up so many good ideas as well as so many bad ones. It had idealism and passion - as a glance at one of the great canvases of J.-L. David will speedily reveal - and it had vision and practical foresight, as its rationalisation of weights and measures also shows.

## A *The August 4th Decrees* [See Doc. 4C(i)]

The contents of this document are more conservative than the renunciations by the deputies or the tone of finality in the opening sentence might imply. The qualifications concerning redemptions and compensation should be noted; likewise the provision for the temporary continuance of certain obligations. Important positive items are the opening of positions to all citizens, and the necessity of providing for the maintenance of the Church now that tithes were to disappear.

The August 4th Decrees should be viewed in the light of the demands of the *cahiers.* They constituted a programme of reform which only time could put into effect, but which, unfortunately, the peasants accepted as a *fait accompli.*

from *Documentary Survey of the French Revolution* by J.H. Stewart, (1951)

## B State Appropriation of Church Functions

(i)  1  Henceforth municipalities shall receive and maintain registers for recording births, deaths and marriages.

2  The councils of the communes shall choose one or more persons from among their members who shall be responsible for such duties.

*Decree* Determining Recording of Vital Statistics, 20 September 1792

(ii)  1  Marriage may be dissolved by divorce.

2  Divorce shall take place by mutual consent of husband and wife...

7  Henceforth, no separation may be pronounced; married parties may be disunited only by divorce.

*Decree* Regulating Divorce, 20 September 1792

## C  Work of the National Convention

(i) The National Convention, numbering among its principal duties that of establishing a new system of public relief on the eternal bases of justice and morality, and considering that it is important that the distribution thereof be made in exact proportion, and in accordance with the most perfect equality that can be attained; having declared as principles, 1st, that every man has a right to his subsistence through work, if he is physically fit, and through free aid if he is incapable of working; 2nd, that the care of providing for the maintenance of the poor is a national obligation, decrees as follows...

*Decree* on Public Relief, 19 March 1793

(ii) The National Convention, convinced that uniformity of weights and measures is one of the greatest benefits it can offer to all French citizens... decrees as follows:

1 The new system of weights and measures, based on the measure of the meridian of the earth and decimal division, shall be used uniformly throughout the entire Republic...

[Appended to the Decree was a table of the new weights and measures, with their equivalents under the old system The point of departure was one-quarter of the meridian, or the distance from the pole to the equator. The basic unit of linear measurement was the ten-millionth part of this quarter-meridian, known as the metre.]

*Decree* Establishing a Uniform System of Weights and Measures, 9 October 1793

(iii) 1    The French Era shall date from the establishment of the Republic on 22 September 1792, of the common era...

2    The common era is abolished for civil uses...

7    The year shall be divided into twelve equal months, of thirty days each, after which five days, not belonging to any month, follow to complete the ordinary year; such days shall be called *complementary days.*

8    Each month shall be divided into three equal parts of ten days each, called décades, and distinguished from one another as first, second and third...

11 The day, from midnight to midnight, shall be divided into ten parts, or hours, each part into ten others, and so on, up to the smallest portion of its duration. The hundredth part of the hour shall be called the decimal minute; the hundredth part of the minute shall be called the decimal second.

*Decree* Establishing the French Era, 5 October 1793

(iv) 9 The names of the days of the décade shall be: primidi, duodi, tridi, quartidi, quintidi, sextidi, septidi, octidi, nonidi, décadi.

The names of the months shall be: for the Autumn, vendémiaire, brumaire, frimaire; for the Winter, nivôse, pluviôse, ventôse; for the Spring, germinal, floréal, prairial; for the Summer, messidor, thermidor, fructidor.

The last five days shall be called the *sans-culottides.*

10 The ordinary year shall receive one day more, as the position of the equinox necessitates, in order to maintain the coincidence of the civil year with the celestial movements. Said day, called *Revolution Day,* shall be placed at the end of the year, and shall constitute the sixth of the *sans-culottides.*

*Decree* Establishing the New Calendar, 24 November 1793

(v) 1    Education is free.

2    It shall be public.

3   Citizens who wish to enjoy the privilege of teaching shall be required:
1st to declare to the municipality or commune that they intend to open a school;
2nd to designate the kind of science or art they intend to teach;
3rd to produce a certificate of patriotism and morality...

*Decree* Concerning Public Education, 19 December 1793

**D   Work of the Thermidorians and the Directory**
(i) The great and enduring work of the Convention was in the field of education... and much of it took place under the Thermidorians. Outstanding items were a Conservatory of Arts and Crafts, Normal Schools,[1] Primary Schools, Central Schools, a Conservatory of Music, and Schools of Public Services e.g. of public works. The establishment of a School of Oriental Languages and a Bureau of Longitudes (a reorganisation of the old School of Mines), and the creation of a National Institute at the summit of the entire educational structure, are but a few of the other representative endeavours in this direction.
Note 1. That is, Teacher-training Colleges, or Colleges of Education.

from *Documentary Survey of the French Revolution* by J.H. Stewart (1951)

(ii) The Executive Directory... deeming it necessary to anticipate difficulties which might result from the application to public accountancy of computation by francs and fractions thereof, decrees:
    1   The two tables annexed to the present decree, the first establishing the value of the franc in terms of the livre tournois, and the second establishing such latter value with the former, shall serve as a basis and rule for public accounts...
    2   Money, either of copper or of bell metal alloyed with copper... shall be used in receipts and expenditures...
    3   The Minister of Finance shall be responsible for the execution of the present decree.
[There follow the two tables; The first established the franc as equal to 1 livre, 3 deniers; the second shows that 1 sou = 0.05 centime, 1 livre = 99 centimes and 100 livres = 98 fr. 77 centimes.]

*Decree* on Francs and Livres, 18 October 1799

# E  Artistic Achievements of the Revolution

**(i) Marat, murdered in his bath, by Jacques-Louis David**

(ii) David's portrait of Bonaparte, crossing the Alps in 1796

## F   Revolutionary Culture and the 'New Man'

One of the critical cultural facts of the Revolution is the attempt to replace the ubiquitous influence of the Catholic Church, inextricably linked to the structures of a dying feudal society, with a more rational, utilitarian form of religion. The most revolutionary event of the 1790s was the introduction of the revolutionary calendar. The new world which was to be inhabited by the new man would now begin with the birth of the Republic, not with the birth of Christ. 'Revolutionary Man' would be secularised from birth; that event, like his marriage and death, would henceforth be recorded in revolutionary days, months and years, in the registers of town halls, not in the Gregorian divisions of time employed in the parish church. The real radicalism of the French Revolution arose from its challenge to the spiritual life of the French people... The brief, and politically disastrous, dechristianisation campaign during the autumn and winter of 1793-94 was regarded by many as the final stage in the creation of the new revolutionary man. The poet Chénier teamed up with the composer Gossec to compose his anthem, the *Hymn to Liberty,* for the ceremony on 10 November 1793, when the cathedral of Notre Dame was rededicated to the worship of Reason. From an élitist standpoint, dechristianisation can legitimately be viewed as the logical outcome of the materialist philosophy of the Enlightenment...

If the 'new man' was to be created in the revolutionary church, the schoolroom was to be the second station on the revolutionary cross. The Constituent Assembly was too busy with the momentous problems of reshaping the constitutional, religious and economic affairs of the nation to deal at length with education, but its successor, the Legislative Assembly, created a Committee on Public Instruction under the chairmanship of the last of the *philosophes,* Condorcet. His project, presented to the Assembly just as war was being declared, was far too voluntary, élitist, not to say idealistic, for the increasingly radical and egalitarian times... Thermidor represents a significant change of direction towards a more practical, élitist policy...

A related expansion in printing and publishing was evident in the 1790s: in 1789, 36 printer-publishers and 194 publisher-booksellers were at work in the capital; a decade later, the number had tripled. The first 'press barons' were born... The concept of 'author' was being transformed from that of a clerk for the transmission of ideas handed down from God... to the notion that ideas were 'individual', the product of individual genius. The law of 19 July 1793 gave legal recognition to this development, granting authors rights to their works during their lifetimes, and to their heirs for ten years after their death...

Move into the public sphere of architecture and we find this same concern for the creation of a new cultural order, for a new physical environment suitable for the new revolutionary man... However, what strikes one most forcibly is the lack of originality and creative innovation, antiquity exercising a powerful influence over artists and architects alike. Verly's columns do offer a hint of 'modernism', but in general, the Doric column, the obelisk and the rotunda win hands down... Political instability, war and financial constraints provide the main explanations for the pathetic physical legacy of the revolutionary era. It is ironic that the French Revolution, whose impact was felt world-wide, should have left so little evidence of its existence...

It is true that, following the downfall of the Jacobins, the revolutionary élite made a determined and successful attempt to exclude the popular masses from the political scene... There was a 'cultural Thermidor' which reflected the failure of the revolutionary élite to embrace the entire nation within its chill, marble neo-classical embrace. Robespierre's attempt, through the Cult of the Supreme Being, to create a 'popular God, a God of the people' ended in an intellectual cul-de-sac. In the field of education, the children of the lower orders were returned to the Catholic fold, whilst those of the 'notables' went on to higher things. France was well on the road from an aristocratic to a bourgeois meritocratic society.

from *The French Revolution: Rethinking the Debate* by Gwynne Lewis (1993)

# Questions

1 Do you agree with J.H. Stewart's views in Source A on the 4 August Decrees? Refer back to Source 4C(i) to support your answer.

**(6 marks)**

2 Which of the decrees in Sources C(i) to C(v) was likely to have aroused the greatest resentment and opposition in France? Explain why. **(6 marks)**

3 How far would you agree that David's works in Sources E(i) and E(ii) were propagandist? **(6 marks)**

4 How far does the evidence of Sources A-E support the view that the years 1789-99 saw social change in France so rapid and far-reaching that it can only be described as a social revolution? **(10 marks)**

5 How important a contribution to the debate on the social achievements of the French Revolution is made by Gwynne Lewis in Source F? Explain your answer. **(12 marks)**

# 13 WOMEN IN THE FRENCH REVOLUTION

Many of the women of the French Revolution remain shadowy, anonymous figures, as inexplicable as the spectral knitting-women who sat at the foot of the guillotine. The lives of the vast majority of women revolved around their husbands, their children and their domestic duties. Very few were rich enough, or influential enough, to make much impact on the course of events. Of these, we have selected three.

The Queen, Marie Antoinette, commonly dismissed as 'that Austrian woman', was the focus of some of the mistrust of foreigners existing in France at this time. Young and spoiled she may have been with her hundreds of dresses and pairs of shoes, but whether she was as empty-headed as she is supposed to have been is still open to question. She found herself condemned for her husband's shortcomings, though she protested that her role had been no more than purely domestic one; she went on reiterating this even at her final trial, but her defence did not keep her from the guillotine.

Madame Jeanne Manon Roland was the wife of M. Roland, one of the moderate politicians of the Constituent Assembly and Minister of the Interior for most of the time between March 1792 and January 1793. He was a leading opponent of the Jacobins in the struggle for power going on at this time, and it was commonly believed that his wife was the main driving force behind him. She was a disciple of Rousseau, and fashionable Parisians of the day considered it an honour to attend the salons she held for the discussion of current issues. When the mob turned against the moderates in 1793 she was arrested and tried by the Revolutionary Tribunal. She was guillotined in November 1793. Her husband killed himself when he heard of her death.

Mlle. Charlotte Corday, a minor noblewoman from rural Normandy and an opponent of Jacobinism, gained a brief notoriety in July 1793 by her attack on the fanatical Parisian revolutionary Marat. Travelling to Paris, she bought a butcher's knife on the eve of Bastille Day and drove to Marat's lodgings, where she stabbed him through the heart. She made no attempt to escape, or to deny the murder. She was brought before the Revolutionary Tribunal, condemned and executed. She, too, seemed to be a fanatic, claiming that she acted in response to voices sent to her by God; but what struck many of her contemporaries was her extraordinary serenity during her last days, and her ironic comment: 'We Parisians are such fine Republicans that no one can understand how a useless female, who could do no good by going on living, could sacrifice herself to save her country.'

But ordinary women did play some part in the Revolution. The famous March of the Women to Versailles in October 1789, though organised and led by men, had substantial female support. A small, noisy minority took part in street demonstrations, and a few even tried to join the National Guard. Only a tiny minority agitated directly for women's political rights; political feminism remained the preserve of Girondin women such as Etta Palm d'Aelders and Olympe de Gouges. Jacobin feminism was more informal. It was the work of the Society of Revolutionary Republican Women, led by Pauline Léon and Claire Lacombe. From the church of St Eustache, they commanded considerable working-class support - though in 1793 they conflicted violently with the market women of the Halles Centrales. Prices and wages were amongst their chief concerns, but there were others almost as important. In the end, however, feminism made little permanent mark on the Revolution.

## A The Queen and the Revolution

(i) The Queen's allowance has been doubled, and yet she has contracted debts... The Queen has bought many diamonds, and her card-playing has become very costly; she no longer plays at games in which the loss is necessarily limited. The ladies and the courtiers are dismayed and distressed by the losses to which they expose themselves in order to make court to the Queen.

The Austrian Ambassador in a letter to the Queen's mother, Maria Theresa, 1776

(ii) The King thinks that the strait prison where he is held and the complete degradation to which the National Assembly has brought the Crown in no longer allowing it to act independently is well enough known by the foreign powers not to warrant any explanation here...

The King thinks that open force, even after a first declaration, would be of incalculable danger, not only for himself and his family, but for all the Frenchmen within the kingdom who do not follow in the path of revolution.

He desires that the fact of the King's captivity be well established and known to foreign powers; he desires that the good will of his relatives, friends, allies and other sovereigns who would wish to concur in its expression be made manifest by a kind of congress to pursue the path of negotiations, with the understanding that there would be an impressive military force to implement them, but always held in reserve so as not to give provocation for crime and massacre.

Marie Antoinette in her instructions to Axel de Fersen before Varennes, July 1791

(iii) *Public Prosecutor:* Where did you get the money to have the little

Trianon built and furnished, where you gave great parties at which
you were always the goddess?
*The Queen:* There were funds specially for that purpose.
*Prosecutor:* The funds were evidently large, for the little Trianon must
have cost an immense amount?
Queen: It is possible that the little Trianon cost immense sums,
perhaps more than I would have wished. We gradually became
involved in more expense. I am more anxious than anyone that what
happened there should be known...
*Prosecutor:* It seems to be proved, despite your denials, that through
your influence you made the former King, your husband, do whatever
you wanted.
*Queen:* There is a great difference between advising that something
should be done and having it carried out.
*Prosecutor:* You made use of the King's weak character to make him
carry out many evil deeds.
*Queen:* I never knew him to have the sort of character you describe...
No one has uttered anything positive against me. I conclude by
observing that I was only the wife of Louis XVI and I was bound to
conform to his will.

Marie Antoinette's examination before the Revolutionary Tribunal, October
1793, as reported in the *Acts of the Tribunal,* ed. G. Walter (1968)

**B   Mme. Roland dies for her moderate beliefs**
(i) After the September Massacres, Mme. Roland hated and feared the
city of Paris. She hated it with especial venom because, as she
believed, it was dominated by her enemy Danton...
    What makes the quarrel between Mme. Roland and Danton so
deplorable is that their dispute need, on a private level, never have
taken place. They had much in common. Both were 'French' to the
marrow of their bones... Both were strong and vigorous personalities;
both were persons of moral and physical courage, a quality they
admired in others.

(ii) Mme. Roland's turn [to be executed] came on 8 November, and
whatever differences had once divided them, Danton cannot have
heard the news with any pleasure.
    She died bravely, after the Roman fashion. Perhaps she had
Charlotte Corday in mind. Mme. Roland had been in prison when the
steely assassin of Marat went to her death, but she had had the event
described to her. Her comment on Charlotte Corday expresses
perfectly her disgust with the Revolution and her contempt for the
persons who now dominated it: 'Charlotte Corday was a heroine
worthy of a better time. I no longer wish to leave prison except to
die.' The night before she died she penned the last sentence of those

memoirs that she had been writing secretly in prison. 'Nature, open your arms,' she wrote. 'God of justice, receive me! At the age of thirty-nine!'

Both extracts from *Paris in the Terror, 1793-94* by Stanley Loomis (1964)

## C  Charlotte Corday murders Marat in his bath-tub

(i) *Public Prosecutor:* What was the purpose of your trip to Paris?
*Charlotte Corday:* To kill Marat.
*Prosecutor:* What motive determined you to do such a terrible thing?
*Corday:* His crimes.
*Prosecutor:* Of what crimes do you accuse him?
*Corday:* The desolation of France and the civil war he kindled throughout the kingdom.
*Prosecutor:* On what do you base this answer?
*Corday:* The man's past crimes were an index of his present ones. He was responsible for the September Massacres. In order to become dictator he lit the fires of civil war. He violated the sovereignty of the people this last June by causing members of the Convention to be expelled and arrested...
*Prosecutor:* How did you kill him?
*Corday:* With a knife I bought at the Palais Royal. I drove it through his chest.
*Prosecutor:* Did you believe that in doing this you would kill him?
*Corday:* That was certainly my intention.
*Prosecutor:* So atrocious a deed could not have been committed by a woman your age. Someone must have incited you to do it.
*Corday:* I told my plans to no one. I was not killing a man, but a wild beast that was devouring the French people...
*Prosecutor:* It is inconceivable that a person of your age and sex could have planned such an act. You must have been inspired by other people, whom you are unwilling to identify, namely Duperret and others who are publicly known to have been Marat's enemies.
*Corday:* How little you understand the human heart! It is far easier to carry out a plan such as this when inspired by one's own hatred than when one is inspired by the hatred of other people.

Charlotte Corday's examination before the Revolutionary Tribunal, July 1793

(ii) I have no pity for the enemies of my country; they have spilled, and continue to spill, the blood of my brothers, who all demand vengeance, and those who have played the part of counter-revolutionaries deserve death at angry hands... I have just been through the department of Calvados, which is far from being republicanized... there in the commune of Caen I fancy I saw all the knives of the partisans of Corday being sharpened, ready to assassinate the patriots.

Letter from a soldier serving in the revolutionary army in Caen, 1793

## D   The End of the Society of Revolutionary Republican Women, October 1793

The Club appears to have been founded originally as an offshoot of the Fraternal Society of Both Sexes, which sat in the same premises as the Jacobin Club, and until August 1793 the Republican Women continued to hold their sessions in the old library of the Jacobin Friary. The new offshoot was restricted to women alone. The affairs of the Club were therefore unique in that they were conducted solely by women, without a hint of the customary subordination to an all-male guiding committee.

At the beginning of August 1793 the Club moved its headquarters to the crypt of the centrally-situated church of Saint-Eustache... The move brought the Revolutionary Women new and disturbing neighbours, for only a public square separated Saint-Eustache from the Halles Centrales, the great central Paris markets with their teeming population of peasant women, stall-keepers and fish-wives, women of a tough plebeian stamp... Wartime dislocations, coupled with the Jacobin economic policy of price control, starved the markets of food-stuffs and other essential trade goods. Zealous section adminis-trators, waging a constant guerrilla war against food speculators and black marketeers naturally found petty market stall-keepers easier targets than the big operators. It was not long before the two factions were embroiled in a bitter feud. The *casus belli* was the apparently insignificant issue of whether or not women should wear the sans-culotte emblem, the tricolour cockade or rosette which had long since been universally adopted by men. On 12 September the Revolutionary Women complained of being attacked, molested and insulted by the market women for wearing the cockade. During the next few days, rioting spread all over the city... The struggle culmina-ted on 19 September in a kind of pitched battle between the rival parties. The ultimate result was a costly victory for the Republican Women...

The hostility of the defeated faction, the market women, continued to smoulder beneath the surface, and was fanned to fresh fury as the Revolutionary Women threw their weight behind the enforcement of the general *Maximum* of 29 September, and a projected house-to-house search to uncover hidden goods. On 28 October this simmering hatred erupted into open violence... In an orgy of revenge, the 'citizenesses' were savagely attacked, and beaten frequently into unconsciousness. This catastrophe meant the end of the Revolutionary Women's Club... The astonishing result was a general decree of the Convention, formally closing all women's clubs in the capital. When a delegation of the Revolutionary Women appeared on 5 November to demand the repeal of this measure, they were howled down by the deputies. The Revolution had finally and irreversibly decided against feminism.

It is difficult to escape the conclusion that the attack on the Revolutionary Women's Club... was inspired and encouraged by Robespierrist elements anxious to carry further the liquidation of the *enragé* opposition already begun in September. By October the Club and its leaders, Pauline Léon and Claire Lacombe, had shown their open hostility to the developing Jacobin dictatorship, and their support for *enragé* policies and programmes. On the other hand, much of the support for the suppression of the Society of Revolutionary Republican Women must have stemmed from less rational motives; in fact, from a deep and abiding anti-feminist prejudice which affected Jacobin revolutionaries no less than other men of their time and place...

The historical importance of the career of Pauline Léon rests uniquely upon her creation of the Society of Revolutionary Republican Women. She left no considered programme of feminism, nor was such a programme ever elaborated in the milieu in which she moved. It remains true, however, that the Revolutionary Women were responsible for bringing the demands of women for political equality before the public for the first time in a dramatic and impressive form.

from *The Enragés* by R.B. Rose (1965)

# Questions

1 (a) How far would you agree that the charges levelled against the Queen in Source A(i) were damaging ones? **(5 marks)**

(b) Do you regard Source A(i) as a reliable source? Explain your answer. **(4 marks)**

2 How far does Source A(ii) confirm or deny the relationship with the King claimed by Marie Antoinette in Source A(iii)? **(4 marks)**

3 Refer to Source B(i), and to your own knowledge, to explain why Danton was Mme Roland's enemy. **(4 marks)**

4 How does Source C(ii) show the importance of Charlotte Corday's crime to the revolutionary cause? **(4 marks)**

5 Fouquier-Tinville, the Revolutionary Tribunal's Public Prosecutor, gained a reputation for bias and for badgering the accused during their trials. How far do Sources A(iii) and C(i) support this view? **(8 marks)**

6 'The three women who are the subjects of Sources A-C had nothing in common except the inevitability of their executions at the hands of the revolutionaries.' Using the Sources A-C, and your own knowledge, assess the truth of this statement.　　　**(6 marks)**

7 How far do Sources A-D explain why women made only a minor impact on the course of the French Revolution?　　　**(10 marks)**

# 14 THE HISTORIOGRAPHY
## OF THE FRENCH REVOLUTION

There is no such thing as impartial history: the story we receive is always to some degree contaminated by the interpretation put on it by the historian. In some cases it would not be too much to say that this interpretation tells us as much about the historian himself as it does about the history he is writing. This is true in the case of histories of the French Revolution, just as it is true in other cases.

When Jules Michelet produced his great seminal work, he was writing in 1847 after eight years of research. In temperament, Michelet was romantic, and consequently gave what might be said to be the orthodox view of the misery and suffering which accompanied the Revolution [See Document 2B(i)]. Furthermore he was living in a period - the later days of Louis Philippe - when the French monarchy was perhaps even more unpopular than it had been in 1789. His account of the situation in France is tinged by this hindsight.

The same is true of Alexis de Tocqueville, whose book on the Revolution appeared in 1856. In his desire to understand the unstable and violent tenor of French life during his lifetime, he turned to the *Ancien Régime* to see what features of it justified the disruption which the Revolution had brought into French life. His view contrasted markedly with Michelet's [See Document 2B(ii)]. He pointed out that by contrast with the peasants of other parts of Europe, the French peasant was in many cases a landowner and relatively well-off. He went so far as to say that the remaining seigneurial obligations were not specially onerous, even though they were deeply resented. Yet Michelet's account remained the generally accepted one.

Hippolyte Taine produced his book in 1875. The catastrophic fall of Napoleon III's Empire had just taken place, and Frenchmen were living in the shadow of the Franco-Prussian War and the political uncertainty of the early days of what was to become the Third Republic. Taine had already made his name in literature and philosophy, and now tried to show his contemporaries the futility of all revolution. He broadly agreed with Michelet that the years down to 1789 were ones of misery and degradation; where he differed was in condemning the Revolution and the violence to which it had led. To him revolution meant disaster, which, far from 'liberating' France, for a time surrendered it to passion and violence. He identified the 'people' with the 'mob', and his anti-democratic sentiments were very obvious to his contemporaries.

The first professional historian to devote most of his life to a study of the documents of the French Revolution, Alphonse Aulard, gave lectures at the Sorbonne in 1912-13, after the Third Republic had been in existence for about forty years, and went out of his way to refute Taine, particularly in his condemnation of the popular features of the Revolution. He showed that the burden of taxation under the *ancien régime* was not excessive, and that violence was not as common as Taine had believed. Aulard was writing in a fairly tranquil era and was a staunch defender of republican ideals against attacks by conservatives like Taine on the right, and the new school of emerging Marxists on the left.

Though not himself a communist, Albert Mathiez was the leading Marxist historian of the 1920s, holding consistently to the view that the Revolution was essentially the work of the powerful and energetic bourgeois class, taking over economic control as the result of the rise of capitalism, and then wishing to extend its dominance to the social and political spheres, where its ambitions were currently thwarted by the existing structure of the *ancien régime*. He showed a typical Marxist hostility to the bourgeoisie, and questioned the high-mindedness of its ideals and actions at all points. His work set the tone for others of similar persuasion, such as Soboul, until the Marxist interpretation became the current orthodoxy for the mid-twentieth century.

So prevalent did the Marxist interpretation become that more than one anti-Communist historian tried to attack Communism by attacking and condemning the Revolution. Pierre Gaxotte was such a historian. Writing in the 1930s, he regarded the Revolution as a disaster from beginning to end, saying that conditions under the *ancien régime* were far from intolerable, and that a few adjustments would have averted the bloody expedients of the 1790s. It is odd that he was able to reach these conclusions as the result of borrowing heavily from the findings of Mathiez, Lefebvre and other left-wing historians, whose conclusions were exactly the opposite of his own.

The collapse of the Soviet experiment after 1990 has gone some way towards discrediting Marxist historians, as the last extract shows. Marxist arguments tend to be shaped sometimes in terms of invincible simplicity, at others of quite byzantine complexity; but generally the political absolutism of the Soviet system has been reflected in the intellectual absoluteness of the Marxist argument. The weakening of the one has led in recent years to the progressive modification of the other.

## A  Was a Revolution Necessary?

Examine administrative correspondence for the last thirty years preceding the Revolution. Countless statements reveal excessive suffering, even when not terminating in fury... People evidently live from day to day; whenever the crop proves poor they lack bread. In many places even an ordinary winter suffices to bring on distress...

Misery begets bitterness in a man; but ownership coupled with misery renders him still more bitter. He may have submitted to indigence, but not to spoliation, which is the situation of the peasant in 1789, for, during the eighteenth century, he had become the possessor of land. The fact is almost incredible, but it is nevertheless true. We can only explain it by the character of the French peasant, by his sobriety, his tenacity, his hereditary passion for property and especially for that of the soil... This is the mode by which the seigneurial system gradually crumbles away and decreases. Towards the last, in many places, with the exception of the chateau and the small adjoining farm, which brings in two or three thousand francs a year, nothing is left to the seigneur but his feudal dues; the rest of the soil belongs to the peasantry... The number of rural holdings is always on the increase. Necker says there is 'an immensity of them.' Arthur Young is astonished at their great number and 'inclines to think they form one-third of the kingdom.'

The small cultivator, however, in becoming a possessor of the soil assumes its charges...Tax collectors, peasants like himself, know how much his property, exposed to view, brings in; they take all they can lay their hands on. Vainly has he laboured with renewed energy; his hands remain as empty, and, at the end of the year he discovers that his field has produced him nothing. The more he acquires and produces the more burdensome the taxes become...

Theoretically, through humanity and good sense, there is doubtless a desire to relieve the peasant. But, in practice, through necessity and routine, he is treated according to Cardinal Richelieu's precept, as a beast of burden to which oats are measured out for fear that he shall become too strong and kick - 'a mule which, accustomed to his load, is spoiled more by long repose than by work.'

from *The Ancien Régime* by H.A. Taine (1875)

## B  Improving Conditions in the Eighteenth Century
There is no question but that personal obligations became less burdensome during the reign of Louis XVI, being specifically lightened... as a result of the edict of August 1779 by which he abolished serfdom on his royal domain...

And so a small part of the feudal burden was lifted from the shoulders of some. Accordingly, overall, the feudal burden was less heavy in 1789, on the eve of the Revolution, than in 1778...

Was there a lightening of the burden in the sense that the seigneurs were less rigorous in demanding the payment of seigneurial dues?...

There were, on the eve of the Revolution, some great seigneurs who were not hard on their tenants, who collected their feudal dues with moderation and who were compassionate to the poor and miserable...

What we are sure of, however, is that if during the reign of Louis XVI the peasants complained very much more than formerly about their feudal obligations, it was because these obligations appeared to them to be less bearable than in former times...

Very many of the land registers *(terriers)* of the seigneurs were revised during the reign of Louis XVI and especially between the years 1780 and 1789... There is little question but that the renewal of the *terriers* increased the revenues of many seigneurs. In some cases the tenants, used to paying little, were very unhappy and complained that they were being asked for more than they owed - when in reality they were perhaps being asked only for what they really owed and nothing more...

The same is true in connection with the ecclesiastical tithe. When the cahiers complain that it had been increased, they do not prove it, or make a very weak case.

It is evident that there is no certainty as to the degree of the increase in the burden of feudal obligations under Louis XVI, if indeed it was increased at all. Perhaps it was actually no heavier, but the peasant was simply less resigned to it.

from *Studies and Lessons on the French Revolution* by Alphonse Aulard (1913)

## C Was the Working Class the Motive Force of the French Revolution?

The Revolution could only come from above. The working classes, whose narrow horizons embraced nothing beyond their calling, were incapable of initiating it, still less of taking the control into their own hands. Industry on a large scale was in its first beginning. Nowhere did the workmen form coherent groups. Those who were on the books of the *corporations,* and subordinate to them, were split up into rival workmen's associations, more interested in petty squabbling than in presenting a united front to their employers. They hoped, moreover, to become employers in their turn and had a chance of doing so, since craftsmanship on a small scale was still the normal form of industrial production. As for the rest, those who were beginning to be employed in the 'manufactories', many of them were peasants who regarded what they earned in industrial employment as a supplement to their agricultural earnings. Most of them were docile and respectful to the employers who provided them with work, so much so that in 1789 they looked upon them as their natural representatives... There was sometimes agitation among them, but they did not as yet feel themselves to be a distinct class of the third estate.

The peasants were the beasts of burden of this society. Tithes, rents in money and in kind, forced labour, royal taxes, service in the militia, all these burdens fell upon them...

Workmen and peasants were capable of a brief moment of revolt when the yoke became too heavy, but could not see their way towards changing the social order. They were only just beginning to learn to read. But they had among them the priest and the local lawyer, who defended their interests in the courts... The country lawyer, obliged as he was by the exigencies of his profession to search among the old feudal deeds could not fail to arrive at a just estimate of the archaic titles which formed the basis of wealth and oppression. It was in the exercise of his profession as feudal expert that Babeuf learnt his contempt for property. He pitied the peasants from whom the greed of their lord set to work to extort fresh dues which had become obsolete.

Thus criticism was working underground which long preceded and prepared for the explosion. The opportunity had only to arise, and all this accumulated and stifled rage would lend force to the attacks of these poor wretches, stirred up and directed by a host of malcontents.

from *The French Revolution* by Albert Mathiez (1928). This extract follows on from Source 2B(iv)

### D Another Historian Takes a Different View

Distress may cause riots, but cannot cause revolutions. These latter are due more to deep-lying causes, and in 1789 the French were not in distress. On the contrary, there is most trustworthy documentary evidence that the country had considerably increased in wealth since the middle of the century and that, with the exception of the country gentry, the material condition of all classes had sensibly improved...

Rousseau once lost his way in the mountains, and, being very hungry, went to a peasant's cottage and asked for something to eat. The man refused. He protested that he had nothing, that everything had been taken from him, that there was not a morsel of food, and that, search as he might, his cupboard was empty. Rousseau begged, insisted, and mentioned his name. The other grew calmer, and, being reassured, tremblingly opened a secret store from which, with an air of great mystery, he produced bread, meat and wine, protesting all the while that he would be lost 'if anyone were to know that he possessed so much wealth.'

from *The French Revolution* by Pierre Gaxotte (1932)

### E Is Marxist History 'Old Hat'?

It is now thirty years since Alfred Cobban, the 'father of revisionism', published his short book, *The Social Interpretation of the French Revolution*, provoking a fierce reaction from Marxist historians. Cobban's attack was directed not so much against the importance of social and economic history as against the imposition of determinist historical (that is, Marxist) laws of development. It is revealing that the socialist historian Georges Lefebvre came out relatively unscathed compared with the onslaught directed against the 'Marxist-Leninist' Albert Soboul. The attack upon Soboul reveals the implicit, often explicit, agenda of many revisionist historians - the rejection of the idea that *revolutionary* action advances the cause of 'progress', whether 'bourgeois' action during the English Civil War and the French Revolution, or 'peasant-proletarian' action during the Russian and Chinese revolutions of the present century. The collapse of the Communist system in Europe over the past few years appears to have provided revisionists with a historical justification for their anti-Marxist approach. Alfred Cobban rejected the notion that revolution was the essential midwife of the new bourgeois society in 1789, hence his emphasis of the economic failure of the Revolution. In other words, revolutions actually impede, rather than advance, the capitalist process which, Professor Cobban agreed, had been developing in Europe over the previous three or four centuries. However, many present-day revisionist historians are, at best, only the illegitimate offspring of their father, placing far less emphasis than Cobban did on the importance of the social and the economic. For these historians, semiotics[1] is more important than social history, old style.

Note 1. Semiotics = the use of empty symbols in language to convey a meaning.

from Gwynne Lewis, *The French Revolution: Rethinking the Debate* (1993)

# Questions

1 Identify the areas of agreement and the areas of disagreement between Sources A and B. **(6 marks)**

2 How far, and in what ways, does the view put forward in Source D challenge the views put forward in Source C? **(8 marks)**

3 Does your study of the French Revolution support Cobban's views, referred to in Source E, that change is not necessarily synonymous with progress? **(8 marks)**

4 From your own knowledge explain what you understand by the Marxist interpretation of the French Revolution. **(8 marks)**

5 Referring to at least two of these sources, explain the difficulties of any historian in attempting to write objective history. **(10 marks)**

# DEALING WITH EXAMINATION

# QUESTIONS

## *Specimen Source-based Question Answer*

(See page 28)

1 How convincingly does the Tiers Etat justify the exceeding of its legal powers in Sources A(i) and A(ii)? **(6 marks)**

The Third Estate puts up a powerful case in Source A(i). It justifies its actions on the grounds that it represents the vast majority of the nation, and that the 'work of national restoration' requires it. But it makes assumptions: it ignores the separate (and lawful?) verification by the nobility and asserts as self-evident that representation is 'one and indivisible.' In Source A(ii) it goes further and, without proof, claims that it has been summoned to 'establish the constitution' - a claim that Louis XVI would have thought preposterous. It conveniently ignores tradition and precedent, and makes unsubstantiated claims. Even so, it justifies itself in strongly emotive and self-confident terms, and the central argument that the Third Estate represents the nation would have been enough to convince most Frenchmen.

2 In the light of his statements made in Sources B(i) and B(ii), what criticisms can be made of the King's leadership during the early stages of the Revolution? **(8 marks)**

The King's appeal to legality in B(i) was entirely justifiable, but it took for granted his ability to coerce the Third Estate into acquiescence. The time for that had been a month earlier, at the time the Estates General had been opened. By mid-June, the Third Estate had formulated a policy and was well led. Unless the King was prepared, and was able, to use force, he could not expect to be obeyed. Thus in B(i) he appears to have made a dubious decision which would be strongly challenged and difficult to enforce. Worse was the reversal of policy, within four days, in Source B(ii). This showed the King as vacillating and indecisive. He justifies his change of heart on the grounds of 'upholding the well-being of my Kingdom', but in effect appears to show weakness in giving in to pressure, whatever his private motives may have been. The politicians of the Third Estate had got the King's measure, and Louis appeared to have lost control of events.

3 Using the sources and your own knowledge, assess how far the changes in Source C represented a revolution. **(10 marks)**

Change is either evolutionary or revolutionary. Where it takes place in so short a time as that of the French Revolution, it can hardly be called evolutionary. The sweeping abolition of feudalism in C(i) marks an important watershed: it may be that feudalism was already, in pre-revolutionary France, being overtaken by developing capitalism, and that the nobility hastened to abandon their dues in order to preserve their property rights; it may be that the safeguards that were built into the measure in almost every clause showed a keenness to salvage as much as possible from the wreck; but the change from a hierarchical society to one based on wealth turned all Frenchmen, peasants, artisans and nobility alike, into 'citizens.' The same radicalism can be seen in C(ii) and C(iii), the one dealing with the individual rights, the other the political rights of the French nation; both are grand and sonorous, though both share the same naivety common to rationalists, that something has only to be defined in order to be achieved. It is true that the decree on Electoral Assemblies (C(iv)) created a special class of 'active' citizens - those who could vote - amounting to some four million only (well under half of France's adult male population). But the unfranchised were not permanently excluded; if they changed their occupation or increased their earnings they could theoretically qualify. The *ancien régime* was perhaps not so *ancien* as some historians, anxious to heighten the pre- and post-1789 contrast, would have us believe; but in a short space of a few months enormous changes had been set on foot, and it would be difficult not to label them as revolutionary.

4   'Source D is more useful to the historian than Source E.' To what extent do you agree?                                         **(6 marks)**

Both sources are accounts not by Frenchmen but by foreigners, and D is an eyewitness's account. Their usefulness will depend on their reliability and factual accuracy, and upon their bias, which in itself could provide historians with valuable clues about contemporary attitudes. Source D conveys the general excitement at the fall of the Bastille; Source E gives a specific and emotive account of the October Days, mentioning the role of named individuals. Rigby seems mildly in sympathy with the events described yet preserves an air of detachment, and is not necessarily himself party to the 'frantic joy' and the 'rapturous joy' he refers to. Mrs. Swinburne reveals her horror of the event in the overall tone of her description and in her reference to 'dreadful doings', 'set of wretches', 'fishwives' and 'bullies.' Her prejudice does not automatically make her account unreliable, but she was not an eyewitness. It really depends on what the historian is looking for: D is more objective, E more specifically informative, though both are by independent observers. If D has the edge, it is because, in this particular instance, the eyewitness account is of greater interest than well-known events reported at second or third hand.

5   Does the evidence in Sources A-F give greater support to the views expressed in Source G(i) or to those of Source G(ii)?                **(10 marks)**

G(i) argues that from July 1789 the Revolution was essentially a popular revolution drawing its strength from the 'urban masses' and the 'bourgeoisie' of Paris and the provincial towns. G(ii) suggests that the Revolution was the work of a wealthy 'propertied élite' whose concern was as much to defend property as to advocate liberty. The popular aspects of the Revolution are demonstrated to a limited extent in C with the abolition of feudalism and the tithe, the 'immense crowd' of D, and the 'wretches', 'fishwives' and 'bullies' of E. Source F, too, refers to a 50 000 crowd of the 'poorer sections of the population.'

But the tenor of the sources is more strongly in support of G(ii). Sources A and B would support both, in that G(i) does not date the popular revolution until July. Source C, however, is full of limitations on a popular revolution: the redeemability of dues and other safeguards in (i) confirm their caution; the modest and timid constitutional arrangements in (iii) and the careful restriction of the right to vote in (iv). The dissatisfaction of the petitioners in F(i) is directed against the legislators, and in particular to 'refractory deputies'; whilst the revolution was so far from being a popular one that the authorities were still prepared (F(ii)) to declare martial law and fire on a 'peaceful and unarmed crowd.' The defence of property is more hinted at than explicit, but the élite is very much present in these sources. The very fact that some of the sources tend to support G(i) is in itself evidence of the serious contradictions between 'rhetoric' and 'reality' which form the central theme of G(ii)'s argument. At the same time it should be noted that the contradictions between G(i) and G(ii) are more apparent than real. Whilst G(i) says that the Revolution was the product of the 'urban masses', it goes on in the next sentence to admit that it was also 'the revolt of the bourgeoisie', many of whom were 'not yet reluctant to become involved.' It does not have the same focus on 'PROPERTY' as G(ii), but this concluding statement goes some way towards narrowing the gap between them.

# Approaching Essay Questions

The key to writing successful essay answers, in the examination room or out of it, must always be relevance to the question set. Relevance is worth much more than length or complexity of detail. Accurate knowledge is also important, but only if it is used as evidence to back up a particular argument. Pure narrative, even of an accurate kind, is much less valuable than material pointed effectively to the focus of a question. Narrative, without analysis, or prepared answers to a topic which do not meet the requirements of the specific question set, are probably the commonest failings of examination answers. Conversely, the best answers are often concise, always relevant, closely analytical and show evidence of wide and thoughtful reading. They concentrate on the thrust of the question, and they arrange and present their arguments coherently, logically and effectively.

Every essay will have a *theme*, i.e. a central historical topic, and a focus, i.e.

the central specific analysis required. Thus, in the question: 'Had internal or external forces the greater influence in creating political extremism in France in the period 1789-94?', the theme is political extremism in France, but the focus is whether its causes were more internal or more external. It is vitally important to notice the theme/focus nature of essay questions. Some students seize on the theme and ignore the focus, producing answers which are often largely irrelevant, or which, if they do hit the target in places, do so rather by accident than by design. A useful test is to cover up the title of an essay written some time ago and see if you can work out an approximation of the title. If you can identify only the theme, but not the focus, then the answer was not a particularly strong one.

## Planning the Essay

The planning of an examination essay should be done quickly, for most of the effort must go into writing the essay itself. In planning the scale of the work, you must have in mind the amount you are actually capable of writing in the time allowed. Within these limits you must plan to make your treatment as comprehensive as possible. First, you should take the title and work out its theme and focus. In every case, you should shape your preparatory material to the focus of the essay, rather than offering a loose approach to the theme in order to include material which you happen to have prepared. Then the shape of the essay itself should be planned. Sometimes a few pencilled words - or even a diagrammatic plan - will suffice. What is *not* needed is a lengthy plan which seriously detracts from the time available for the essay itself.

## The Shape of the Essay

The essay should fall into three distinguishable parts:

1 **Introduction.** If you have thought out what you intend to say it should not be too difficult to introduce your argument and how, generally, you propose to develop it. The more punchy your introduction, the more it will engage the attention of the reader. The danger, unfortunately, is that students often seem obliged to resort to lengthy 'background' material which serves little purpose. They sometimes take refuge in the stratagem of: 'Before answering this question, it is first necessary to...'. It is better to have no introduction at all than one of this sort.

2 **The body of the essay.** This should develop your case fully. Each paragraph should make a particular point in the argument. Paragraphs should not be too long and should be logically linked to the paragraph preceding. If you study a well-written essay, you will find link-words such as 'Moreover', 'Nevertheless' and 'However', or phrases such as 'On the other hand...'. These are worked into the text to give it a logical structure. The idea behind the linkage is to lead the reader smoothly from one stage of the argument to the next in a sensible, orderly flow.

3   **The conclusion.** This should draw together the threads of the argument
    and bring it to a logical end. Obviously, the more conclusive the argument,
    the fewer loose ends and unanswered questions will be left. Unfortunately,
    in practice, many conclusions turn out to be tiresome repetitions of what
    has just been written, and thus lack the force they should have. It is better
    to have no conclusion at all than one of this sort.

## *Types of Essay*

1   **List questions** usually require a list of factors of one sort or another -
    usually causes, results or features. You may be asked to 'explain' why Louis
    XVI was deposed, or what were the 'effects' or 'consequences' of the Coup
    d'État of Thermidor. Or you may be asked to 'explain in what ways' the
    French Revolution became more extreme. List questions may ask directly
    for the evidence supporting or refuting a particular viewpoint, as for
    example: '"The French Revolution brought about great social and
    economic change in France." What evidence supports this view?' In such a
    case, the evidence selected has to be set out.

2   **'How far'** or **'To what extent'** questions ask you to consider the relative
    significance of a given person or event in a particular historical situation.
    You may be asked: 'To what extent did political extremism take hold of
    France in the 1790s?'; or you may be presented with a quotation such as
    '"War made the Terror inevitable." How far do you agree?' All such
    questions demand analysis, evaluation and historical judgment.

3   **Comparison questions.** These appear in different guises. It may be a
    comparison of two politicians or statesmen, e.g. Danton and Robespierre,
    or it may be a comparison of policies e.g. those of the Girondins and the
    Jacobins. Whichever it is, a point-by-point comparison is far more effective
    than treating the two to be compared one after the other. Occasionally you
    may be asked to 'Compare and contrast'. In fact there is little difference
    between the two; the first, literally, means 'find the similarities', and the
    second 'find the differences', but in practice it is difficult to do the one
    without doing the other.

4   **Judgment** or **'Yes/No'** questions. These are very popular with examiners.
    A judgment on some person or event is presented to support or otherwise.
    It may be suggested to you that "The French Revolution was the outcome
    of practical needs rather than of political theories" and you may be asked
    to 'discuss', 'comment on' or 'consider' this verdict. You may even be
    asked 'Do you agree?'. At their simplest, such questions may be answered
    in a single word, 'Yes' or 'No', though answers of such brevity are not to be
    recommended! In nearly all instances a balanced approach will be needed.
    You may be able to support the judgment up to a point, but will have
    reservations which you will develop. Perhaps the judgment cannot be
    supported. Then you will have to prove this to be the case. Never assume

that you are expected to give a judgment unqualified support; but remember that in History, categorical statements are nearly always capable of some challenge.

In tackling most history questions a variety of different approaches are perfectly possible. For this reason, 'model' answers should be treated with some caution. Most examiners will admit not only that some of the best work they have seen is short and pithy, but that the best essays sometimes plot an unexpected course to an answer. Answers which contain an element of surprise start off with the distinct advantage of engaging the interest of the examiner; if they sustain this advantage through their own merits the candidate is well on the road to success.

There are books available which deal in some depth with the issues connected with question analysis and essay preparation. Students may find some of the following useful:

C. Brasher, *The Young Historian,* (OUP, 1970)
J. Cloake, V. Crinnon & S. Harrison, *The Modern History Manual,* (Framework Press, 1987)
J. Fines, *Studying to Succeed - History at A-level and Beyond,* (Longman, 1986)
D.M. Sturley, *The Study of History,* (Longmans Green, 1969)

The following list of essay titles on the French Revolution includes suggestions - no more than suggestions - on how to approach them, plus a specimen answer for one of them. Use them as part of your course or for examination practice.

## Possible Essay Titles

The essay titles given below are modelled on the A-level questions set by a number of Examining Boards. The answers that follow are intended as general guidance for students; they are not the only ways in which the questions can be answered.

1    Do you agree that the French Revolution was the outcome of practical needs rather than of political theories? *(Type 4)*

This is not a bland question on the causes of the French Revolution, but requires a sharp focus on the practical and theoretical aspects of the causes. Revolutions are seldom brought about by abstract ideals; it is usually necessary for the advocates of revolution to adopt a few ideals in order to provide a little moral drapery to cover their actions. Thus, in 1788-89, aristocrats, parliamentarians and the representatives of the non-privileged classes talked much about liberty and rights while pursuing their own self-interest. So whilst the crown was concerned about possible state bankruptcy, the privileged classes were busy undermining absolutism in order to strengthen their own positions, whilst posing as defenders of France's liberties. Meanwhile the poor were increasingly restless in the face of a worsening economic situation. Rousseau and the other philosophers would have been horrified to see how the revolutionaries put philosophic ideas into practice; but in alerting Frenchmen to their 'rights' they had undermined the consensus that reform could only come from above, providing the unprivileged classes with a reason for remedying their grievances. You might well argue that 'practical needs' were the motivating factor, but that the invoking of 'political theories' provided a significant justification.

2   To what extent was the French Revolution caused by economic distress? *(Type 2)*

Once again, an unfocused rehearsal of 'the causes of the French Revolution' would be inadequate. The focus is on the importance of 'economic distress' as a cause. You ought to be able to dismiss peasant discontent at the outset. Certainly there was much economic distress, but the peasants became revolutionary only briefly during the Great Fear and the August Days, and both these came after the political revolution was well under way. The 1780s were difficult times, both for the monarchy and for the privileged classes, but the difficulty arose from financial stringency, not from economic distress. Insofar as there was actual poverty, it helped to fill the towns with the starving and the unemployed, useful material to be ignited by the revolutionary mobs. But the importance of this has been scaled down recently. Marxist historians have tended to emphasise the importance of 'economic distress' as part of their relatively fixed view of history; but if the initial impetus came from above rather than below, the main causes will have to be sought elsewhere.

3   Why was the Estates General summoned to meet in 1789, and what was the importance of this summons in bringing about the French Revolution? *(Type 1)*

This appears to be a straightforward question on causes; but note that here we are getting two questions for the price of one, both of them focusing on the summoning of the Estates General. For the first part, avoid narratives of the 1780s or even earlier. Focus on the national financial and fiscal emergency, and on the failure of a succession of ministers to resolve it. Those who sought a shift of power from king to aristocracy and parlements used every device, and especially the Assembly of Notables, to thwart the royal will and to force the summoning of the Estates General, which they then planned to use to their own advantage.

   The second part can be linked to the first by leading on to the failure of the privileged classes to manipulate the Estates General for their own purposes. Once they declared their attachment to the forms of 1614, the Third Estate realised that the aims of the First and Second Estates were not the same as their own. Necker also recognised this, and made a belated attempt in the 'Result of the Council' to rescue the situation by giving the Third Estate 'double' representation, though he did not achieve its logical counterpart - joint session. As it was, the King could easily have survived; but his ministers' failure to formulate a clear programme of reform, together with his fatal dithering over whether the Estates should be allowed to sit together, brought growing impatience and disrespect from the National Assembly.

You should also briefly consider how the meeting of the Estates General is also linked to the breakdown of law and order, in Paris and the countryside, both potent factors in turning what had been intended as a political bluff into a full-scale revolution.

4   At what stage in 1789 did the situation in France become a Revolution? *(Type 4)*

This is a judgment question in that you are being asked for your own judgment in selecting the point at which revolution began. The danger is the narrative approach - a résumé of events and a snap judgment. It might be best to avoid pure chronology, and deal with political and social change separately. You could argue that only when the revolution was both political and social could it be said that France was 'in a state of revolution.' Thus the meeting of the Estates General was not in itself revolutionary; it was more a revival of tradition to deal with an exceptional situation. Not until the King surrendered to the Third Estate in late June was a political revolution under way. Likewise, the revolution in the countryside did not really begin until the taking-over of landed estates in the Great Fear of July. You might alternatively put up a good case in arguing for e.g. the fall of the Bastille, or the October March of the Women as the crucial occasion.

5   Why did France fail to find a stable government between 1789 and 1792, after the Ancien Régime had been destroyed? *(Type 1)*

The theme is France, 1789-92, but the focus is on reasons why France failed to find a stable government during that time. Among the factors which need to be discussed will be the separation of powers introduced in 1790 and confirmed by the Constitution of 1791; the King's alienation from the Revolution by the Civil Constitution of the Clergy, and the delay in finalising the new constitution until after the Flight to Varennes, when his rejection of the Revolution was clearly demonstrated. The inexperience of the politicians was compounded by the self-denying gamble of rival politicians in the Constituent Assembly. The increasing influence of the Clubs and the growing Republican movement were both politically destabilising. The task of promoting national reform was too great for the succession of mediocre ministers to whom Louis XVI entrusted the government, and in whom he had little confidence. The subsequent attempt of the government to strengthen its position by embarking on a war failed abysmally. Overall it might be argued that the monarchy, the executive and the legislature were all pulling in different directions during these years, and it is hardly surprising that a stable government failed to emerge.

6  'He could not effect reform, nor would he accept it.' How far does this
   statement explain the failure of Louis XVI both as an absolute and
   constitutional monarch? *(Type 2)*

While historians have argued over Louis's guilt or innocence at his trial, there
has been no attempt to revise the long-held judgment that he was politically
inept. He was not strong enough to break free from the customary procedures
in which he had been enmeshed since his accession. Theoretically absolute,
Louis should have been able to cut his way clear from the tangle and embark
upon policies of his own; but his intellect was as second-rate as his advisers',
and he remained trapped in his problem. The King's vacillation, his failure to
give a strong lead, his failure to call the bluff of the parlements were all crucial
to the failure of fiscal reform from above in the 1780s. Worse still, having
allowed himself to be manoeuvred into calling the Estates General, Louis had
no clear policy on how it should function or what reforms it should be invited
to sanction. In most ways, it was a policy of drift, and during the crucial
months Louis wavered uncertainly between suppression and concession, and
lost the initiative.

His failure as a constitutional monarch is not exclusively his own fault; with
constitutional monarchs it never is. Nor is it true to say that he could not
accept reform. Louis agreed to the sweeping reforms of 1789, and a good deal
of the reform programme thereafter. He was chiefly obstinate over church
reform, as he thought he should be. But as a constitutional monarch he was
no longer in control of events, and the royal position was untenable long
before Varennes.

It might be worth adding that the paradox implied in the question is not
genuine: Louis XVI was always a constitutional monarch, whether the
constitution was the formal one which he found himself forced to sign in
1791, or whether it was the traditional one under which he and his ancestors
had governed in former years. The notion that he was ever free to please
himself in what he did might have been true of Napoleon but it certainly was
never true of Louis XVI.

7  Why was Louis XVI deposed and later executed during the French
   Revolution? *(Type 1)*

It is important to note the two parts in this question - the reasons for
deposition and for execution are markedly different. Do not make the mistake
of writing a narrative of events, assuming that the reasons will emerge from it.
Nor is it necessary to begin earlier than 1789. You might argue that the King
was personally popular, and that his position as constitutional sovereign
seemed secure enough in the earlier stages of the Revolution; but that his
frequent use of the veto, as over the Civil Constitution of the Clergy, lost him
much goodwill. The election of the Legislative Assembly, from which former
deputies were excluded, in practice strengthened extremism. Furthermore,
war did not, as expected, unite all men in patriotic duty round the King, but

instead highlighted the links that bound the royal family to the national enemy, the Habsburgs. This was exacerbated by the defeats of the summer of 1792, leading directly to the King's deposition.

The second half of the question deals with the King's trial and execution. The trial produced a competition between individuals, all of them under pressure from the public gallery, to show how deeply committed each was to the Revolution. It seemed to the radicals a good idea to compel the moderates to identify themselves by forcing them to vote personally on the issue. But, however much French leaders believed in the sovereignty of the people, they would not allow the question to be settled by a referendum. Perhaps Robespierre came closest to the truth when he said that the execution was brought about by the necessity to make a clean break with the past and 'purify' the Revolution.

8   Why, and in what ways, between 1789 and 1793, did the French Revolution become more extreme? *(Type 1)*

In dealing with 'ways' and 'why' it will be necessary to concentrate in this question on analysis and explanation, and to avoid description. By 'extremism' is usually meant the development of republicanism, the growing influence of the clubs and the use of violence culminating in the Terror. The early steps should be noted in 1789. In 1790-2 we have the rapid rise of the political clubs and the overriding issue of the Civil Constitution of the Clergy, alienating the King from the revolution. The flight to Varennes began the process of rendering the King's position untenable. The political inexperience of the members of the Legislative Assembly strengthened the importance of the Paris-based clubs and of the Commune; whilst failure in war weakened the Brissotins and played into the hands of their extremer rivals. Thus the overthrow of the monarchy was only a matter of time, and led to the emergence of the Jacobins in 1793. Their successful bid to control the Convention in June led to their assuming control of the all-powerful executive committees they had helped to set up, and the elimination of their opponents by instituting the Terror. The reasons for all this do not only lie in the weaknesses that created the possibility for the move towards extremism; there was also a white-hot ideological conviction which drove the revolutionaries along this path. There was to be no resting until the whole rotten edifice of the *ancien régime* was torn down.

It is easiest to see the progress of extremism in the political sphere, but some attention should be given to religious, social and economic changes to make the picture complete - all of them meddling with the traditional order, so as to make it more uniform, rationalistic, comprehensive and efficient.

9   Had internal or external forces the greater influence *in creating political extremism in France in the period 1789-94?* (Type 4)

Here the theme is political extremism, but the focus is on the internal/external forces which brought it about. A non-directed catalogue of causes of extremism will not suffice. You would be on safe ground in arguing that until 1791 the causes of extremism were predominantly internal, and that not until the Flight to Varennes and the Declaration of Pillnitz did the external threat begin to take shape, making patriotism, loyalty to the Revolution and Republicanism synonymous. The advent of war in 1792 was largely instrumental in bringing down the monarchy; whilst war failure in 1793 undermined the Girondins and promoted the Jacobins. The Terror was begun in consequence of internal threats almost as much as the foreign danger; but to many Frenchmen the distinction between counter-revolution and foreign interference was by no means clearcut. That the Terror continued for so long was in part due to the war, but in part to the tactical Jacobin use of it as a justification for suppressing political opposition. It had outlived its usefulness when peace in La Vendée and the battle of Fleurus ended the national emergency.

10 Why did the French Revolution lead to the Terror? *(Type 1)*

This is a straightforward question on cause and consequence. There is a danger that highlighting the principal milestones on the road to the Terror will be long on description and short on explanation. So develop an effective argument. Some historians see the Terror as the inevitable consequence of two things: the breakdown of law and order, and the readiness with which those seeking power resorted to violence. The Revolution was marred with violence from the outset; even during periods of comparative calm violence lurked just below the surface. The political clubs could increase the tension at will through their influence over the Sections, and they revealed their ability to whip up the mob whenever they felt the need. The Girondins attempted to create tighter controls before the Jacobins took power and made them the instruments of the Terror. They had no intention of losing power in the same fashion, and to avert this organised and intensified the Terror to repress their opponents.

Why was there this drift towards lawlessness? Part of the answer lies with the weakness of the King. His indecision sprang not only from natural squeamishness and lack of will, but from the knowledge that many of his troops were disloyal and unreliable. Worse than this, there was a decline in respect for authority in general from the top downwards. Encouraged by half-educated demagogues with a superficial knowledge of fashionable political writings, the lower orders sought to substitute liberty for order, equality for rank and an insolent fraternity for the deference to which they were accustomed. As Edmund Burke was not slow to point out, the corrosion of lawlessness soon dissolved the good along with the bad. Respect for peace, for property and the rights of others, respect for life even, disappeared. By 1794, the fabric of the *ancien régime* had virtually disintegrated. Only courage and resolution, such as was shown at Vendémiaire, would halt the slide into anarchy: that required the talents of a Bonaparte.

11  How much emphasis should be placed on 'violence and extremism' in analysing the progress of the French Revolution from 1789 to 1795? *(Type 2)*

This is not a question confined to violence and extremism: narratives of the Revolution's excesses should be avoided. An analysis of the progress of the Revolution against the background of violence and extremism is required. Thus the extremism in the countryside in the summer of 1789 must be seen against the end of the *ancien régime,* the Rights of Man and similar legislation. 1790 and 1791 were comparatively free of excesses but strong on reform. Although violence and extremism returned in the September Massacres, the King's execution and the Jacobin Terror, this was also a period of reform: of the currency, the tax system, the calendar, schools, weights and measures, and a variety of experiments aimed at creating economic controls. That Jacobinism was extreme in its methods is undeniable, but it was less so in its ideas. The guillotine retains its fascination for all who study the period, but the death-toll was always wildly exaggerated and the phase of violence soon passed; but the fundamental changes made in France by the Revolution proved to be radical and permament.

12  Why was it that, despite internal disturbances, France enjoyed extensive military success from 1792 to 1802? *(Type 1)*

The focus is on the reasons for military success, and a narrative of military campaigns should be avoided. The reference to the internal disturbances suggests that the implied contrast needs attention. Of course, at first in 1792 the French did badly. If this served to turn defence of the Revolution into a patriotic duty, and to discredit decentralised government, paving the way for the Jacobins, then it prepared the ground for later success. In 1793 the French success, continuing over the next few years, was largely assured by the levée en masse made necessary by the risings in Vendée and Lyons; by the brilliant organising ability of Carnot; by the new fighting techniques made necessary by a conscript rather than a professional army, and by the emergence of outstanding officers, rapidly promoted, who were no longer confined to the privileged class. All these things led to Napoleon, and his exceptional use of reconnaissance, artillery, forced marches, and his tactical gifts, contrasted with the weakness and divisions amongst France's enemies and their reliance on eighteenth-century drill books. But France's military supremacy was not absolute: Napoleon failed in Egypt and Marengo was a close call; and at sea it was a vastly different story.

13  'The course of the French Revolution in the years 1792-93 ended the influence of one tyrant and installed another in his place.' Discuss this view of the replacement of Louis XVI by Robespierre. *(Type 4)*

This question makes one wonder firstly whether in fact Louis XVI was directly succeeded by Robespierre, and secondly whether either or both of them was a tyrant. You may suggest that the answer both these questions is in the negative.

The Revolution certainly brought the downfall of the King in 1792, but it would be misleading to describe him as a tyrant. In his supposedly autocratic years Louis XVI had been characterised by his passivity and his ineptitude. His tyranny was a myth fostered by his detractors. The August Days of 1792 ended the monarchy but did not instal Robespierre: as yet he had influence but no power. Louis's trial, in which it was expedient to depict him as a tyrant, strengthened the Jacobins, Robespierre's party. But though the Jacobins came to dominate the Convention, they never had a guaranteed majority in it, and, like Robespierre himself, often found themselves uncomfortably wedged between the Citras in the Convention and the Ultras in Paris, their freedom of action limited. Robespierre dominated the Convention and the Committee of Public Safety but he never had absolute power. He might look like a tyrant, especially to those who had little sympathy with his objectives. But he was always one of a group, and had powerful colleagues like St Just and powerful rivals like Hébert and Danton. War and economic necessity determined the course of the Revolution, not Robespierre; rather than controlling events, he was controlled by them. After Thermidor, it became expedient for former colleagues to throw the whole blame for the Terror on him, thus excusing themselves. To depict him as a tyrant will always to some extent fly in the face of the evidence.

14 'In Robespierre, one sees high social ideals in sharp contrast with crude political methods.' Discuss. *(Type 4)*

[See specimen answer in next section.]

15 'A man for the times.' Account for the rapidity of the rise, and of the fall, of Maximilien Robespierre. *(Type 1)*

This is a question hinging on a quotation. This appears to suggest that what is required is an essay about the appropriateness of Robespierre for the years of his power; yet what is actually asked is something quite different. If you should come across an essay title of this sort, the best thing to do is to ignore the red herring, and obey the instructions which follow.

The question is actually concerned with the reasons for Robespierre's rapid rise, and for his rapid fall. You may well argue that, within the short time-scale of the French Revolution, his rise was no more rapid than that of many other contemporary leaders. His involvement with the Cordeliers and Jacobin Clubs brought him more influence, but power did not come until 1793. Even then he was not undisputed leader, but one of a small inner group of Jacobins who gave France a centralised and almost collective leadership.

His fall was certainly more rapid. It can be attributed mainly to the instability of Parisian politics in 1794. His execution of Hébert and his friends meant that the Sections would no longer respond automatically to the Jacobin call to action, whilst the fall of Danton and the haste and injustice of his trial and execution alienated many who regarded Danton as one of the heroes of the Revolution. His own actions, whether due to discouragement, indecision or merely to physical exhaustion, hastened his fall. The transition from almighty politician to helpless victim was remarkably rapid, and his Thermidorian opponents were surprised by the ease of their success. But none of Robespierre's predecessors had lasted long, and there was no reason why he should be any different.

16  Why did the Directory not arouse more enthusiasm amongst its contemporaries? *(Type 1)*

Compromises seldom inspire enthusiasm, and it is worth exploring how far the Directory was a wartime compromise between the political left and the right. Those in power declared themselves to be Jacobins, but their Jacobinism was much more pragmatic and tentative, and much more out of sympathy with Parisian radicalism, than it had been during the Terror. As the Directory tried to steer a middle course between the two, it was popular neither with the monarchists nor the Jacobins, and its support base was therefore narrow. Repeated rounds of unsatisfactory election results led to disreputable political manoeuvring and ultimately to dependence on the military, making the Directory appear weaker than it was. Its domestic achievements ought to have gained it more respect, but, with the international situation so pressing, its domestic successes seemed only minor. Perhaps the foreign and military successes of the Directory should have received more credit, but even Carnot was eclipsed by the achievements of Jourdan, Moreau, Masséna and Napoleon. When the Directory got into difficulties with the Second Coalition, its reputation was so low that Napoleon thought that few would be able or willing to rally to its support; in any case, for him, it was a window of opportunity. If you want to argue that the Directory did arouse contemporary enthusiasm, you will have some difficulty in proving your case. Contemporaries, whose views were generally reflected by the historians, remained hostile; it has been only recently that historians have attempted to rehabilitate the reputation of the Directory.

17  Did the Jacobins have an economic policy? *(Type 4)*

To agree would be anachronistic. Political parties of the twentieth century may sometimes lay claim to coherent economic policies, but it is difficult enough to label eighteenth-century political groupings as parties, let alone assign specific policies to them. The best that can be done is to see what sort of consensus the Jacobins had on economic matters. There is a lot to be said for the argument that the Revolution was in part a reaction against Mercantilism and Protectionism, which were the current economic dogmas. Quesnay and the Physiocrats exercised a profound influence on the Revolution, and their principles were taken aboard by the Jacobins. Free trade and *laissez faire* meant the removal of restrictions, and favoured the interests of the commercial bourgeoisie. Fiscally, the Jacobins inherited the financial deficit, but could only manage it by the increasing issue of an inflationary paper money. Inflation they unsuccessfully tried to control through a series of laws on price control, each new law an admission that the earlier one had failed. Much argument has been devoted to the social make-up of the Jacobin party. The consensus that it was dominated by the *petits bourgeois* helps to explain its dislike of big business, its idealisation of the independent working man and its loathing of trade unions and similar associations. The Jacobins promoted uniform weights and measures to aid commerce, but had no policies to stimulate the economy generally . They desperately dabbled with piecemeal state directives, though their grasp of economic basics was so primitive that they had no idea how to build a fully-fledged command economy. The situation was made worse by differences of opinion within the party. Robespierre was the champion of the small capitalist; St Just favoured policies of confiscation; Hébert was suspected of populist socialism; Babeuf put forward a naïve programme of communism and he and his followers were guillotined for their pains. Economic disagreement mirrored political disagreement: neither was a substitute for bread. Jacobinism was swept away before France was able to finance economic recovery on the back of foreign plunder - a policy just as economically pragmatic as that of earlier Jacobin experiments.

## *Specimen Essay Answer*

(See page 113)

The answer below is not a model answer, nor does it represent the only approach to the question. Nevertheless, it is an answer which focuses on the question and which represents the type of answer which may be written under examination conditions in 45 minutes.

'In Robespierre, one sees high social ideals in contrast with crude political methods'. Discuss. *(Type 4)*.

Robespierre has been something of an enigma both to his contemporaries and to historians. The paradox presented in the title of the essay derives on the one hand from his reputation as an idealist and on the other from the crudity of his political manoeuvring; that is, from his reputation as a high-minded man - what Carlyle called a 'sea-green incorruptible'- and from his reputation for ruthlessness as principal architect of the Terror. There are other contrasts. He was a man of violent radical beliefs, yet he dressed like a gentleman of the old regime - powdered hair, smart clothes, neat neckwear, and with a dandified, precise manner; he was ruthless and often extremist, yet he was unsure of himself, nervous and withdrawn in company and timid in his personal relationships; he was the subject of passionate urgings, but controlled them rigidly. But perhaps these are false contrasts. There is no paradox between incorruptibility and extremism; to treat them as opposites is an over-simplification. Furthermore, such qualities were not unusual, at the time

**115**

of the revolution: Couthon, St Just, Desmoulins all possessed them to some degree.

Robespierre's idealism was derived partly from his clear thinking and training as a lawyer, but chiefly from his wide and uncritical reading of reformist literature and from the simplicity of his inexperienced political intellect; the appalling crudity of his methods was no worse than that of virtually all his political contemporaries.

Perhaps he is best regarded as a political puritan - a leader who reached, often vainly, for lofty ideals; who grew impatient with those who did not share his ideals; who rejected half-measures or compromise; and who believed that individuals were capable of realising a vast potential if they could only master their own frailties. And, like many idealists, he destroyed himself through his own rigidity.

Robespierre is early depicted as the conscientious lawyer of the ancien régime whose small and unremunerative legal practice brought him a reputation for advanced opinions. Personally squeamish about taking life, he refused to be a judge; not surprisingly he secluded himself in his shuttered house on the day of Louis XVI's execution, and many of his interventions in the work of the Revolutionary Tribunal during the Terror were on the side of clemency.

He entered politics as deputy for Artois in 1789, summing up what he saw as the nation's grievances in his Address ('To the Working-class Nation'). Mirabeau sensed the abstract flavour of his speeches on the rights of man and felt him to be a dangerous maniac whose passionate beliefs and personal ambition might lead the nation to disaster.

The flight to Varennes made Robespierre a republican, in order that the goals of the revolution should not be betrayed by counter-revolution. At first he opposed both war and violence. Later, however, he came to support the war (in spite of the fact that the Girondins, his opponents, were its main instigators). He saw the revolution as a necessary and inevitable stage in the liberation of man. Elected to the Convention, he was soon championing the policies of the Jacobins against Girondism. When war brought extreme foreign danger, Robespierre became convinced that the revolution could be saved only by purging the nation of those who threatened it; yet his refusal to condemn the September Massacres committed him to a theory of popular justice that was little short of lynch-law. When the trial of the King took place, he pressed for the death penalty in spite of his views on capital punishment ('Because the country must live, Louis must die.') Thus Robespierre campaigned for blood-letting and purification. He saw them as a means of cutting out the diseased portion of society; he did not see them in terms of individuals being put to death. His stress on virtue, purity and religion made him unpopular amongst his colleagues, who feared his inquisitorial eye, but he was a valuable member of governing committees and a popular public idol. At the same time, his stress on purification struck hope and fear simultaneously into the hearts of the people ('Without Terror, Virtue is impossible;

without Virtue, Terror is pointless'.)

So social justice was to be achieved at a cost. While danger threatened, purification by guillotine would continue. Danton's proposals for a Committee of Clemency were no less dangerous than sanculottism or Hébert's wild calls for atheism. It is sometimes said that such men threatened Robespierre's own position of control; that social ideals gave him his justification in seeking for power, but love of office made him cling to it; that even the deism to which he adhered seemed almost as much an opportunity to parade himself in his sky-blue suit as an affirmation of the spiritual needs of the nation. But the truth is that Robespierre's character lacked both the cynicism and the brutality of the majority of dictators. There is no reason to doubt that he aimed at political liberty according to his own definition, and saw the revolutionary dictatorship as purely temporary in a time of crisis. He was not the personal tyrant depicted by his opponents of Thermidor.

Robespierre's social ideals did not extend to the economy. His economic thinking, together with that of most of his contemporaries, was largely undeveloped. He believed that the laws of supply and demand could be repealed by the government, and his Law of the Maximum could be made to work. He thought that Paris could be fed if the government exercised the appropriate powers and if the criminals responsible for the shortages were identified and punished. He rejected anything reminiscent of socialism. Generally, he shared the views of the middle class on economic matters. He disapproved equally of the guilds and the trade unions, his uncertainties mirroring those of his mentor Rousseau. But though he appeared to hold private property sacrosanct, he approved a plan for redistributing émigré and clerical lands and did not hesitate to use the Law of the Suspect to reward those who denounced public enemies with their confiscated wealth.

These uncertainties have their parallel in his political methods. At first he was a political novice, groping his way towards a coherent policy via constitutional monarchy and moderate republicanism, but, by 1791, he was more fully aware of the power base his leadership in the Jacobin Club gave to him. Thus there was nothing naive in his support of the Constituent Assembly's self-denying ordinance preventing its members being elected to the Legislative Assembly; the more ineffective the new assembly, the more powerful would become the Jacobin Club. He kept in the background in the autumn of 1792, but when the King's trial had been decided on he was able to make use of the trial to tie those who favoured the King's death firmly to the Jacobin cause, and to impugn those who wanted to save the King with a share in Louis's guilt.

He exercised no dominant authority in the Committee of Public Safety; he was not a permanent member until July 1793, and Barère, Carnot and Prieur signed far more decrees than he did. Nor does he bear the sole responsibility for the intensified Terror of 1794. While he agreed that the enemies of the people deserved death, he was never as severe either as the members of the Committee of General Security or as the more fanatical and repulsive of his colleagues, such as St Just (the 'Angel of Death'). Some of his policy decisions may have been of questionable wisdom. Paying volatile sansculottes to attend Section meetings, and walking the political tightrope by striking simultane-ously at the Left (Hébert) and Right (Danton) were perhaps risky and dangerous decisions. And when in July 1794 he tried to browbeat the Convention by making non-specific threats against unnamed members he was repeating previously successful tactics in a different, more hostile, situation. But the fact remains that historians have perhaps overrated Robespierre's importance on account of the exaggerated attention paid to him by his Thermidorian opponents: Robespierre came to personify the Terror without being fully responsible for it.

In the end the Terror with which he is identified claimed him as a victim. Yet Robespierre would have regarded the Terror only as a means to an end; it was a political system based on fear, but he would have regarded it purely as temporary and not as his sole political method. He was, as French revolution-ary politicians went, more idealist than many, and in his methods a good deal less crude than most.

# BIBLIOGRAPHY

There are a great many books on this well-known subject, and a short list involves a rather subjective choice. The older books have generally been excluded; but some of them still remain so good that their names are included. Most if not all of these texts are still readily available. If you find you do not get on with the one you pick, turn to others; there is a wide choice.

## *Outline Histories*

**William Doyle,** *The Oxford History of the French Revolution,* (OUP, 1989). This is a good one-volume history of the French Revolution. Judicious and well-balanced, the book is revisionist in tone rather than in content.

**A. Goodwin,** *The French Revolution,* (Hutchinson, 5th ed. 1970). Short and compact, but still a classic treatment in its way. Unfortunately the book stops at the fall of Robespierre.

**Ben Jones,** *The French Revolution,* (ULP, 3rd Imp., 1974). Comprehensive treatment to 1799.

**Georges Lefebvre,** *The French Revolution, in two volumes: From its Origins to 1793, & From 1793 to 1799,* (Routledge & Kegan Paul, 1964). Meatier than single-volume histories, but attractively written by an acknowledged expert.

**Gwynne Lewis,** *The French Revolution: Rethinking the Debate,* (Routledge, 1993). From a series called Historical Connections, it presents alternative and up-to-date interpretations of the French Revolution. Best tackled by those who have got a good grounding in the subject matter.

**Simon Schama,** *Citizens: A Chronicle of the French Revolution,* (Penguin, 1989). Long - over 900 pages - but at the same time racy and readable. Excellently illustrated, but dismisses the six years after 1794 as an 'epilogue'.

**Albert Soboul,** *The French Revolution, 1787-1799,* (NLB, 1974) A substantial book by an acknowledged expert, giving comprehensive treatment of the whole period. Marxist in tone.

**J.M. Thompson,** *The French Revolution,* (Basil Blackwell, Oxford, 2nd ed., 5th imp., 1959). Rather old, but still very good. Stops at Thermidor.

**Duncan Townson,** *France in Revolution,* (Hodder & Stoughton, 1990). Concise and well-presented introduction to the subject. Contains useful practical advice and guidance for students.

# Aspects of the Period

**C.B.A. Behrens,** *The Ancien Régime,* (Thames & Hudson, 1967). Quite old, but still excellent and very readable.

**T.C.W. Blanning,** *The French Revolution: Aristocrats v. Bourgeois,* (Macmillan, 1987). Useful material on the conflicts leading to revolution.

**T.C.W. Blanning,** *The Origins of the French Revolutionary Wars,* (Longman, 1986). One of the few books with its focus on the revolutionary wars.

**William Doyle,** *Origins of the French Revolution,* (OUP, revised ed. 1989). An excellent summary of recent research.

**Norman Hampson,** A *Social History of the French Revolution,* (Routledge & Kegan Paul, 1963). Extremely useful, but tails off after 1795.

**P.M. Jones,** *The Peasantry in the French Revolution,* (CUP, 1988). Useful and well-focused.

**Georges Lefebvre,** *The Directory,* (Routledge & Kegan Paul, 11965). Stylish and penetrating.

**Stanley Loomis,** *Paris in the Terror, 1793-94,* (Jonathan Cape, 1964). Written like a thriller.

**Martyn Lyons,** *France under the Directory,* (CUP, 1975). An excellent short account.

**R.R. Palmer,** *Twelve Who Ruled,* (Princeton University Press, 1941). Biographical approach to the Year of Terror; very readable.

**R.B. Rose,** *The Enragés: Socialists of the French Revolution?,* (Sydney University Press, 1965). Unusual and interesting material.

**George Rudé,** *Robespierre: Portrait of a Revolutionary Democrat,* (Collins, 1975). Good biographical treatment, with absorbing detail.

**George Rudé,** *The Crowd in the French Revolution,* (Oxford Clarendon Press, 1959). Still tremendously popular and valuable; concentrates chiefly on the Terror.

**J.M. Thompson,** *Robespierre and the French Revolution,* (EUP, 1952). Shorter biographical treatment, but still good value.

**Michel Vovelle,** *The Fall of the French Monarchy,* (CUP, 1974) Excellent material, but stops in 1793.

**G.A. Williams,** *Artisans and Sans-culottes,* (Libris, reprinted 1989). Together with Rose (above), a useful book.

# INDEX

This is not an exhaustive index, but contains the major references to the personalities and events in this book